DATE DUE

White Writing

Books by J. M. Coetzee

Foe
Life & Times of Michael K
Waiting for the Barbarians
In the Heart of the Country
Dusklands

J. M. Coetzee

White Writing

*On the Culture of Letters
in South Africa*

*Yale University Press
New Haven and London*

Chapter 6 of this book is revised and reprinted from *English Studies in Africa* 23 (1) 1980, pp. 41–58, ©Witwatersrand University Press. Versions of other parts of the book have appeared in: *Social Dynamics* (chapter 1), *English in Africa* (chapters 3 and 5), and *Tijdschrift voor Nederlands en Afrikaans* (chapter 4). Research was funded in part by the Human Sciences Research Council. The conclusions reached are my own and are not to be attributed to the H.S.R.C.

Designed by Nancy Ovedovitz and set in Baskerville type by Huron Valley Graphics, Inc. Printed in the United States of America by Vail-Ballou Press, Binghamton, N.Y.

Library of Congress Cataloging-in-Publication Data

Coetzee, J. M., 1940–
  White writing.
  Bibliography: p.
  Includes index.
  1. South African literature (English)—White authors—History and criticism. 2. Literature and society—South Africa. 3. Landscape in literature. 4. Whites in literature. 5. Race relations in literature. 6. Farm life in literature. 7. Afrikaans literature—History and criticism. I. Title.
PR9358.2.W45C64 1988   820'.9'8034068   87-21568
ISBN 0–300–03974–3 (alk. paper)

The paper in this book meets the guidelines for permanence and durability of the Committee on Production Guidelines for Book Longevity of the Council on Library Resources.

10   9   8   7   6   5   4   3   2   1

Cadmus agit grates peregrinaeque oscula terrae
figit et ignotos montes agrosque salutat.
. . . superas delapsa per auras
Pallas adest motaeque iubet supponere terrae
vipereos dentes, populi incrementa futuri.
—Ovid, *Metamorphoses* 3

[Pressing his lips to foreign soil, greeting the unfamiliar
mountains and plains, Cadmus gave thanks. . . . Descending from above, Pallas told him to plow and sow the earth
with the serpent's teeth, which would grow into a future
nation.]

Contents

Frontispiece from *Naaukeurige en uitvoerige Beschrywing van de Kaap de Goede Hoop* [Detailed and extensive description of the Cape of Good Hope], by Peter Kolbe. 2 volumes (Amsterdam, 1727). The monument is crowned with the emblem of the Dutch East India Company.

Introduction

I

In 1652 a European settlement was planted at the tip of the African continent, at the Cape of Good Hope. It was set there for a specific and limited purpose: to provide fresh produce to East Indiamen trading between the Netherlands and Asia. The Dutch East India Company, which ran the settlement, had little interest in the hinterland of the Cape, which, report said, was barren, inhospitable, and sparsely peopled by primitive Hottentots and Bushmen.[1] Interest waned further when exploring parties failed to find any workable mineral deposits. For the next century and a half, till the colony became a pawn in the great-power rivalry of Britain and France, the Company tried, irresolutely and unsuccessfully, to discourage the spread of settlement into the interior, to hold the colony to what it had originally been planned as: a trading post, a garden.

1. In accord with old-time usage, the usage of almost all the writers I deal with in this book, I employ the words *Hottentot* and *Bushman* instead of the modern *Khoi* and *San*. For the same reason, I sometimes use *Kaffir* for *Xhosa* and *Boer* for *Afrikaner*.

1

One question to ask about these torpid times is, Why did the garden myth, the myth of a return to Eden and innocence, fail to take root in the garden colony of the Cape? For while the promise of a fresh start on a fresh continent deeply affected the shape of history in Europe's New World colonies, in South Africa, in many respects a *lui-lekker land* (land of ease and plenty), the only myth that ever came to exert a comparable animating force was the story of the wanderings of the Israelites in search of a Promised Land, a story of tribal salvation appropriated as their own by the wandering Afrikaner tribes.

The simplest answer to the question is that Africa could never, in the European imagination, be the home of the earthly paradise because Africa was not a new world. The western Eden drew its power from a confluence of circumstances none of which would hold for a rival African paradise. Early explorers of the Americas, particularly of Spanish America but also of Virginia and the Carolinas, were spellbound by the prospect, real or realizable, that, with the discovery of this paradise, the millennium might be upon them. "That release of energies known as the Renaissance was largely stimulated by geographical excitement as interpreted by the myth of Eden," writes Charles Sanford (41): the westward voyage became a voyage into the future of man. The culture, the habits, the general disposition of the Amerindians whom Europeans first encountered induced observers like Bartolomé de las Casas to speculate that here was man in a state of original innocence, a model to his fallen Old World brethren (Queraldo Moreno 118). And the news of a western Eden was diligently broadcast by the poets of the imperial powers, as well as by entrepreneurs like the Hakluyts with a stake in encouraging investment and settlement in the colonies (L. Wright 109; Kolodny 11). The Cape, by contrast, belonged not to the New World but to the farthest extremity of the Old: it was a Lapland of the south, peopled by natives whose way of life occasioned curiosity or disgust but never admiration. It struck neither the trading company that administered it nor the prosperous public of an underpopulated Netherlands as a place with much to offer the settler or the investor.

If the Cape was never claimed to be a terrestrial paradise, even less did it—as did the Puritan colonies of North America—aspire to be a city on a hill serving Europe as an example of true spiritual reformation. In fact, till the coming of the British in 1795, the Cape not only remained a historical backwater but took no part in the great debate—inaugurated so theatrically by Las Casas and Sepúlveda in Valladolid in 1550 and conducted thereafter on two continents and in many tongues—on the responsibilities of Christian Europeans to their new colonial subjects (Hanke 112).

Yet the topos of the garden, the enclosed world entire to itself, is more extensive than the Judaeo-Christian myth of Eden. In its isolation from the great world, walled in by oceans and an unexplored northern wilderness, the colony of the Cape of Good Hope was indeed a kind of garden. But the future promised by the Cape seemed to be less of the perfection of man in a recovered original innocence than of the degeneration of man into brute. Again and again visitors to the colony warned that, from lack of any spur to activity in the economically stagnant hinterland, colonists were declining into the idle and brutish state of the Hottentots. Like Joseph Conrad after them, they were apprehensive that Africa might turn out to be not a Garden but an anti-Garden, a garden ruled over by the serpent, where the wilderness takes root once again in men's hearts. The remedy they prescribed against Africa's insidious corruptions was cheerful toil.

The degeneration of the white colonist in Africa was no peripheral matter to his masters in Europe, in that it threatened one of the arguments by which expansive imperialism justified itself: that those deserve to inherit the earth who make best use of it. Thus in the theory of "double right" propounded by Governor John Winthrop of Massachusetts, the rights of cultivators, who clear and settle the land, always take precedence over the rights of nomads, who merely hunt over it (Tichi 8). The Dutch Boer in Africa was subjected to close and censorious scrutiny (scrutiny that continues to this day) because his sloth, his complacent ignorance, his heartlessness towards the natives, his general slide into barbarism seemed to betray the whole imperial side.

To pastoral art the West has assigned the task of assserting the virtues of the garden—simplicity, peace, immemorial usage—against the vices of the city: luxury, competitiveness, novelty. In the variety known as georgic, the pastoral also holds up the garden in bloom against the garden in decay, the garden degenerating into wilderness. In South Africa pastoral art takes on both these tasks. It is essentially conservative (there is nothing of what Poggioli calls Tolstoyan pastoral, the pastoral of the Left [30]); it looks back, usually in a spirit of nostalgia, to the calm and stability of the farm, a still point mediate between the wilderness of lawless nature and the wilderness of the new cities; it holds up the time of the forefathers as an exemplary age when the garden of myth became actualized in history.

In the literature of such unsettled settlers with so uncertain a future as the whites of South Africa, the retrospective gaze of the pastoral has understandably proved more reassuring than the prospective gaze of its twin genre, the utopia. Pastoral has been a prominent strain in their writing, and never more so than in the 1930s, when, fearing the end of a *boere-nasie* (nation of farmers), as Afrikaners left the land and were swallowed up in the cities, Afrikaans novelists elaborated models of the garden-farm as bastion of trusted feudal values or cradle of a transindividual familial/tribal form of consciousness. Though she wrote in English, Pauline Smith, with her stories of rural Afrikaners tucked away out of sight of history, holding on to their peasant virtues as well as their peasant vices, belongs to this line too.

The great antipastoral writer in South Africa is Olive Schreiner (1855–1920). The farm of Schreiner's *Story of an African Farm*, like the farm of pastoral, seems to lie outside history, outside society. But this is true only to the extent that the Cape Colony itself lies outside history; otherwise the farm mimics the idleness, ignorance, and greed of colonial society. To Schreiner the Cape Colony, and perhaps all colonies, are in truth anti-Gardens, dystopias.

In the idleness of life on her late nineteenth-century farm, the same idleness that outraged John Barrow at the turn of the century, Schreiner underscores the centrality of the question of labour in the South African pastoral. Pastoral in the West has always been under pressure to demonstrate that the retreat it advocates from the business of society is not a mere escape into sensual sloth. Since Virgil it has responded by claiming that the essence of pastoral virtue is a simple life of honest labour:

> [The farmer's] rest is sound, his life devoid of guile . . .
> [He] lives in peace, his children all
> Learn how to work, respect frugality,
> Venerate their fathers and the gods:
> Surely, Justice, as she left the earth,
> In parting left her final traces here.
>
> [*Georgics* 2:467, 472–74]

Pastoral in South Africa therefore has a double tribute to pay. To satisfy the critics of rural retreat, it must portray labour; to satisfy the critics of colonialism, it must portray white labour. What inevitably follows is the occlusion of black labour from the scene: the black man becomes a shadowy presence flitting across the stage now and then to hold a horse or serve a meal. In more ways than one the logic of the pastoral mode itself thus makes the incorporation of the black man—that is, of the black serf, man, woman, or child—into the larger picture embarrassing and difficult. For how can the farm become the pastoral retreat of the black man when it *was* his pastoral home only a generation or two ago? A hut on the white man's farm can be proposed as the just and proper place for the black man only as long as it can be argued that it is a step up from a hut in the wilderness; yet on the farm, where his raison d'être is to perform the work that is the badge of his ascent from the indolence of the wilds, his toil threatens to deprive the white man of the labours that he, as Africa's new heir, must not only perform but, more important, be seen to perform.

The constraints of the genre therefore make silence about the black man the easiest of an uneasy set of options. If the work of hands on a particular patch of earth, digging, ploughing, planting, building, is what inscribes it as the property of its occupiers *by right*, then the hands of black serfs doing the work had better not be seen. Blindness to the colour black is built into South African pastoral. As its central issue the genre prefers to identify the preservation of a (Dutch) peasant rural order, or at least the preservation of the values of that order. In (British) capitalism it identifies the principal enemy of the old ways. Locating the historically significant conflict as between Boer and Briton, it shifts black-white conflict out of sight into a forgotten past or an obscure future.

What was it that pastoral novelists wished to preserve of a rural order that, by the late 1920s, was clearly in crisis? To Pauline Smith (1883–1956) it was a social stability that she idealized, even fabricated. To C. M. van den Heever (1902–57) it was an organic mode of consciousness belonging to a people who, from toiling generation after generation on the family farm, have divested themselves of individuality and become embodiments of an enduring bloodline stretching back into a mythicized past.

Neither of these essentially conservative visions is entirely homegrown. Smith's farm of Harmonie has many of the features of the great country house of the English Tory tradition; Van den Heever owes much to the Romantic earth-mysticism of *Blut und Boden* Germany. The receptivity of Smith and Van den Heever to strains of European reaction, and, in a different and more sinister way, of Sarah Gertrude Millin (1889–1968) to the racial science of the European Right, is an index of the weakness of the liberal-individualist tradition in South Africa, compromised by its association with get-rich-quick exploitation of the country's resources and with the anomie of the boomtowns. It is also an index of the failure of the Left to persuade the new landless white proletariat that its future was linked to that of a growing black proletariat. To the present day, the isolationist romance of the return to the family farm remains part of the dream-fare of the petit-bourgeois descendants of these landless farmers.

II

One dream topography that the South African pastoral projects is therefore of a network of boundaries crisscrossing the surface of the land, marking off thousands of farms, each a separate kingdom ruled over by a benign patriarch with, beneath him, a pyramid of contented and industrious children, grandchildren, and serfs. But there is a rival dream topography as well: of South Africa as a vast, empty, silent space, older than man, older than the dinosaurs whose bones lie bedded in it rocks, and destined to be vast, empty, and unchanged long after man has passed from its face. Under such a conception of Africa—"Africa, oldest of the continents"—the task of the human imagination is to conceive not a social order capable of domesticating the landscape, but any kind of relation at all that consciousness can have with it.

To the pastoral novel, landscape is humanized when inscribed by hand and plough: in effect, the genre invokes a myth in which the earth becomes wife to the husband-man. But to other dream-topographers it is by no means clear that the ploughshare is enough to break the resistance of Africa. To begin with, how much of the soil of Africa is soft enough to plough? To Schreiner and a line of writers after her, Africa is a land of rock and sun, not of soil and water. What relation is it possible for man to have with rock and sun?

This landscape remains alien, impenetrable, until a language is found in which to win it, speak it, represent it. It is no oversimplification to say that landscape art and landscape writing in South Africa from the beginning of the nineteenth century to the middle of the twentieth revolve around the question of finding a language to fit Africa, a language that will be authentically African. Of course there exist plenty of authentically African languages, languages indigenous to the subcontinent. But their authenticity is not necessarily the right authenticity. The quest for an authentic language is pursued within a framework in which language, consciousness, and landscape are interrelated. For the European to learn an African language "from the outside" will therefore not be enough: he must know the language "from the inside" as well, that is, know it "like a native," sharing the mode of consciousness of the people born to it, and to that extent giving up his European identity. So, quite aside from the question of whether it is practical for a European to enter African culture in sufficient depth, quite aside from European doubts about whether the black man anyhow "appreciates" the landscape into which he was born any better than an animal does, the question has to be rephrased: Is there a language in which people of European identity, or if not of European identity then of a highly problematical South African–colonial identity, can speak to Africa and be spoken to by Africa? (This argument pushes the African into an intrinsically double-bound situation: in order to convince the European that he appreciates Africa he must give evidence of a degree of alienation from it; once he is thus alienated he can no longer claim to be by nature at one with it.)

Once we have reformulated the question in this way, we see better why the lone poet in empty space is by no means a peripheral figure in South African writing. In the words he throws out to the landscape, in the echoes he listens for, he is seeking a dialogue with Africa, a reciprocity with Africa, that will allow him an identity better than that of visitor, stranger, transient. It is not surprising, then, that the poetry of landscape should occupy so central a place in the English-language tradition in South Africa. Nor is it surprising that this strain should begin to wane about the time (the 1960s) when, on the one hand, political and cultural ties with England ("home") began to grow thinner and an African nationality, if not an African identity, was in effect imposed upon English-speaking whites, and on the other it began to be apparent that the ultimate fate of whites was going to depend a great deal more urgently on an accommodation with black South Africans than on an accommodation with the South African landscape.

Many English-colonial doubts about cultural identity are projected and blamed upon the English language itself, partly because, as a literary medium, English carries echoes of a very different natural world—a world of downs and fells, oaks and daffodils, robins and badgers—partly because English makes no claim (as Afrikaans does) to being native to Africa, partly because of the mystique, promoted by emigré teachers with a stake in maintaining a special status, that English is spoken correctly only in southeast England, and then only by a certain social class, partly because the writer's audience is split between colonials with whom he has some community of experience and metropolitans to whom so much has to be explained that he inevitably lapses into exasperated simplifications. But dissatisfaction with English would in truth hold for any other language, since the language being sought after is a natural or Adamic language, one in which Africa will naturally express itself, that is to say, a language in which there is no split between signifier and signified, and things are their names.

From this essentialist conception of language we see why it is that one of the preoccupations of English-language poetry, down to Sydney Clouts, should be with the interiority of things, with the heart of the landscape, its rocks and stones, rather than with what decks its surface. What response do rocks and stones make to the poet who urges them to utter their true names? As we might expect, it is silence. Indeed, so self-evidently foredoomed is the quest that we may ask why it persists so long. The answer is perhaps that the failure of the listening imagination to intuit the true language of Africa, the continued apprehension of silence (by the poet) or blankness (by the painter), stands for, or stands in the place of, another failure, by no means inevitable: a failure to imagine a peopled landscape, an inability to conceive a society in South Africa in which there is a place for the self. In this respect the art of empty landscape is the pessimistic obverse of a wishful pastoral art that by the labour of hands makes the landscape speak, and peoples it with an ideal community.

(Wishful, perhaps, but not extravagantly wishful; if the pastoral writer mythologizes the earth as a mother, it is more often than not as a harsh, dry mother without curves or hollows, infertile, unwilling to welcome her children back even when they ask to be buried in her, or as a mother cowed by the blows of the cruel sun-father. Not surprisingly, in the farm novel we find women, in effect, imprisoned in the farmhouse, confined to the breast-function of giving food to men, cut off from the outdoors. Schreiner's Tant' Sannie, the greedy, cruel, selfish, man-eating matriarch, is a prescient attack upon the servant stereotype even before the stereotype has come to be written down.)

The literature of empty landscape (and here I would include Schreiner's novel) is thus a literature of failure, of the failure of the historical imagination. The poet scans the landscape with his hermeneutic gaze, but it remains trackless, refuses to emerge into meaningfulness as a landscape of signs. He speaks, but the stones are silent, will not come to life. Or when this is not true, when the stones seem on the point of coming to life, they do so in the form of some giant or monster from the past, wordless but breathing vengeance. In the poetry of monsters under the earth we see the return of what is repressed in the poetry of the silent landscape, in the silence that is read upon (that is, once the disguise is stripped off, written on to) the landscape as well as being read out of it: what Roy Campbell calls "the curbed ferocity of beaten tribes" (129).

III

I have two concerns in this book: with certain of the ideas, the great intellectual schemas, through which South Africa has been thought by Europe; and with the land itself, South Africa as landscape and landed property.

The first of the European ideas I address is the idea of Man, which the Hottentots in the early years of the Colony in certain respects so puzzlingly and troublesomely failed to live up to (chapter 1). The second is the idea of cultural progress, the idea that cultures can be ranged along a scale of evolutionary ascent from "backward" to "advanced." Through this schema the European enabled himself to see in South Africa, layered synchronically one on top of another as in an archaeological site, hunters, pastoralists, early agriculturists, advanced precapitalist peasant agriculturists, and even agriculturists in the process of regressing to nomadic pastoralism, all of whom, belonging to "simpler" stages of evolution, could be understood as "simple" people thinking simple thoughts in their various simple languages (chapter 5). Another is the idea that, mankind being "naturally" divided into distinct races, sexual unions that cross racial lines are unnatural and yield degenerate offspring (chapter 6). A fourth is the idea that, when people are "at home in" or "at harmony with" a particular landscape, that landscape speaks to them and is understood by them (chapters 2 and 7). All of these ideas, deployed with a degree of blind force in proportion as they were held at various times to be self-evident, undeniable, "natural," constituted part of the repertoire of thinking by which Europe held sway over a faroff, interesting, but finally unimportant part of the world.

The Hottentots failed to live up to the idea of Man because they did, or seemed to do, so little with their time. To the science of Man, the spectacle of wholesale idleness is inherently scandalous. But the spectacle of native labour in South Africa, always more or less involuntary, never adequately rewarded, has its own scandalous force. The literature of white pastoral (discussed in chapters 3, 4, and 5) marks off for itself, and defends, a territory "outside" history where the disturbing realities of land and labour can be bracketed off, and questions of justice and power translated into questions of legal succession and personal relations between masters and servants. Like the black corpse in Nadine Gordimer's novel *The Conservationist* that keeps floating up out of the earth, however, doubts about the pastoral enterprise keep floating up, till in the end they subvert the genre. Was there no time before the time of the forefathers, and whose was the land then? Do white hands truly pick the fruit, reap the grain, milk the cows, shear the sheep in these bucolic retreats? Who truly creates wealth?

By the end of World War II the economy of the Union of South Africa had shifted definitively from a rural to an urban base. In 1948 a party of Afrikaner nationalists came to power and began to sever political and cultural ties with Europe; as apartheid began to be implemented, moral ties were severed too; and from being the dubious colonial children of a far-off motherland, white South Africans graduated to uneasy possession of their own, less and less transigent internal colony.

The essays making up this book barely touch on this new, neocolonial period of South Africa's history and the literature it gave rise to. Even within their temporal limits, they do not constitute a history of white writing, nor even the outline of such a history. Nor does the phrase *white writing* imply the existence of a body of writing different in nature from black writing. White writing is white only insofar as it is generated by the concerns of people no longer European, not yet African.

1

Idleness in South Africa

I

The local natives have everything in common with the dumb cattle, barring their human nature.... [They] are handicapped in their speech, clucking like turkey-cocks or like the people of Alpine Germany who have developed goitre by drinking the hard snow-water.... Their food consists of herbs, cattle, wild animals and fish. The animals are eaten together with their internal organs. Having been shaken out a little, the intestines are not washed, but as soon as the animal has been slaughtered or discovered, these are eaten raw, skin and all.... A number of them will sleep together in the veld, making no difference between men and women.... They all smell fiercely, as can be noticed at a distance of more than twelve feet against the wind, and they also give the appearance of never having washed.

The above observations on the Hottentots of the Cape of Good Hope were compiled in 1652—the year of European settlement of the Cape—by the Amsterdam publishing house of Jodocus Hondius, from travellers' reports (Hondius 26–28). Through its display of footnotes, its maps, its engravings of Hottentots in exemplary poses, Hondius's little book seems to wish to emphasize that it is no work of fantasy: everything it records has truly been witnessed. Within the limits of the veracious, however, the picture it presents of the Hottentots is a selective one. The facts we read about them are above all remarkable facts, selected by the writers of the original reports from the mass of impressions they received at the Cape for being remarkable, and picked out in turn by Hondius because they seem likely to strike the man in the street in the same way.

In the early records one finds a repertoire of remarkable facts about the Hottentots repeated again and again: their implosives ("turkey-gobbling"), their eating of unwashed intestines, their use of animal fat to smear their bodies, their habit of wrapping dried entrails around their necks, peculiarities of the pudenda of their women, their inability to conceive of God, their incorrigible indolence. Though many of these items are merely copied from one book to another, we must believe that in some cases they were rediscovered or confirmed at first hand. They constitute some of the more obvious *differences* between the Hottentot and the West European, or at least the West European as he imagined himself to be.

Yet while they are certainly differences, these items are perceived and conceived within a framework of *samenesses,* a framework that derives from the generally accepted thesis enunciated at the opening of the extract from Hondius above: that although the Hottentots may seem to be no more than beasts, they are in fact men. Hottentot society being a human society, it must be amenable to description within a framework common to all human societies. The categories and subcategories of this framework will constitute samenesses extending across all societies. They will be the universals, while particular observations inserted in the various slots will constitute the differentia that mark particular societies.

Although the framework of categories within which the travel writers operate is nowhere explicitly set forth by them, it is not hard to extract it from their texts. The list is something like the following:

1. Physical appearance
2. Dress: (a) clothing, (b) ornamentation, (c) cosmetics
3. Diet: (a) foodstuffs, (b) cuisine
4. Medicine
5. Crafts: (a) handicrafts, (b) implements
6. Technics
7. Weapons
8. Defence and warfare
9. Recreations
10. Customs
11. Habitation: (a) dwellings, (b) village layout
12. Religion (including superstition, witchcraft, magic)
13. Laws
14. Economy
15. Government
16. Foreign relations
17. Trade
18. Language
19. Character

Though the number of categories employed may not be nineteen in each case, behind each of the discourses called "Account of the Hottentots" or "Description of the Hottentots" exists some such grid. At its most immediate level, the grid functions as a compositional aid, giving a form of arrangement to the data. But at another level the grid functions as a conceptual scheme, and as such creates the danger that observations may be deformed to fit into one slot or another when they "really" cut across the categories, or that things that belong in no preconceived slot will simply not be seen. Thus—to give hypothetical examples—observations of drug-induced trances and prophecies might fall under Medicine or Religion or (possibly) Law or Government, but decidedly not under all four; observations of cattle-slaughtering rituals under Diet or Dress or Religion or (possibly) Economy, but not under all four. Or, to give real examples, we find O. F. Mentzel pondering over whether the Hottentots' so-called *Pisplechtigheid* (ceremonial urinating) is a recreation or a religious ceremony, or adducing it as proof of the poverty of the Hottentots' language that they use a single term (translated as *andersmaken*) to cover the acts of marrying a couple, initiating a youth into manhood, curing an illness, and driving out a spirit (Mentzel 2:281, 288).

Of course it is too much to expect of the seamen, ships' doctors, and Company officials who contribute to what I will henceforth loosely call the Discourse of the Cape that they will put aside their inherited Eurocentric conceptual schemes in favour of a scheme based on native conceptual categories. Such a move would be entirely anachronistic. But it might further be said that the collapse of the categories of (say) Diet, Medicine, and Religion into each other would threaten to collapse systematic discourse into what the traveller started with: a series of sightings and observations selected from sense-data only on the grounds that they are striking, remarkable; that is to say, into a mere *narrative* rather than a comprehensive *description*.

The crippling weakness of anthropological narrative as compared with anthropological description is that, in reverting to chronological sequence, it forgoes access to the achronological, spatial, God's-eye organization of categorical description. Some travel writers try to have the best of both worlds—the immediacy of narrative, the synopticism of description—by disguising the latter as the former. Here, for example, is Christopher Fryke writing of a visit to the Cape in 1685:

> My curiosity led me to enter one of [their huts] and see what kind of life these people led. As I came within, I saw a parcel of them lying together like so many hogs, and fast asleep; but as soon as they were aware of me, they sprang up and came to me, making a noise like turkeys. I was not a little concerned; yet seeing that they did not go about to do me any harm, I pulled out a piece of tobacco and gave it to them. They were mightily pleased, and to show their gratitude they lifted up those flaps of sheepskin which hang before their privy-parts, to give me a sight of them. I made all haste to be gone, because of the nasty stench; also I could readily perceive that there was nothing special to be seen there. Moreover, some I found at their eating, which made the stink yet more unbearable, since they had only a piece of cow-hide, laid out upon the coals a-broiling, and they had squeezed the dung out of the guts, and

smeared it with their hands over one another. And the hide they take out when it is broiled, and beat it, and so eat it. This so turned my stomach, that I made haste to be gone. [Raven-Hart, *CGH* 2:259]

The historical veracity of this narrative is much to be doubted (a few pages later Fryke comes upon a serpent eating a Hottentot). But note how the brief story is put together by the stringing together of anthropological commonplaces from the categories Physical Appearance, Dress, Diet, Recreations, Customs, Habitation, Language, and Character:

1. The Hottentots sleep by day (idle Hottentot character) in a hut (Hottentot dwelling), lying all over one another (Hottentot sexual mores) like hogs (place of Hottentots on the scale of creation).
2. They make a noise like turkeys (Hottentot language).
3. They accept tobacco (Hottentot recreations) and lift their flaps (Hottentot dress) to exhibit (Hottentot sexual more) their private parts (anatomical peculiarities of the Hottentots).
4. Fryke is driven away by the stench (Hottentot uncleanliness), observing as he leaves Hottentots smearing one another with dung (Hottentot cosmetics) and eating cowhide and guts (Hottentot diet).

One of the commonplaces of the Discourse of the Cape is that the Hottentots are idle. Since it is not custom but absence of custom, not recreation but absence of recreation, this idleness usually finds its place in category 19 as part of Hottentot character. Surprisingly little mention of Hottentot idleness occurs in the approximately 150 accounts that R. Raven-Hart summarizes from travellers who touched at the Cape before 1652.[1] But as the Company begins to settle in and accounts of the Hottentots become more detailed, the theme becomes more prominent, idleness being described and denounced in the same breath.

1. Only three travellers mention idleness, and all three deduce the idleness of the Hottentots from the fact that they did not practise agriculture, rather than observing it: Edward Terry, 1616; Augustin de Beaulieu, 1622; and Johan Wurffbain, 1646 (Raven-Hart, *BVR* 83, 101, 165).

They are lazier than the tortoises which they hunt and eat.—Johan Nieuhof, 1654 [Raven-Hart, *CGH* 1:22]

They are a lazy and grimy people who will not work. . . . They are idle, and like to sit without doing anything.—Volquart Iversen, 1667 [Raven-Hart, *CGH* 1:103]

Their chief work is nothing more than to dig up and eat . . . roots. . . . When they are satiated they lie down without a care.—George Meister, 1667 [Raven-Hart, *CGH* 1:203]

The major work of the men is to lie about, unless hunger drives them.—Johann Schreyer, 1679 [L'Honoré Naber 40]

If they are not hungry, they will not work.—Christopher Fryke, 1681 [Raven-Hart, *CGH* 2:234]

They are very lazy, liking better to go hungry than to work.—Fr.-T. de Choisy, 1685 [Raven-Hart, *CGH* 2:269]

They secure for themselves a luxurious idleness, they never till the soil, they sow nothing, they reap nothing, they take no heed what they shall eat and drink. . . . Whoever wishes to employ them as slaves must keep them hungry.—William ten Rhyne, 1686 [Schapera 123]

They are a very lazy sort of people. . . . They choose rather to live . . . poor and miserable, than to be at pains for plenty.—William Dampier, 1691 [Raven-Hart, *CGH* 2:385]

Their native inclination to idleness and a careless life, will scarce admit of either force or reward for reclaiming them from that innate lethargic humour.—John Ovington, 1693 [Raven-Hart, *CGH* 2:396]

They are extremely lazy, and had rather undergo almost famine, than apply themselves.—Francois Leguat, 1698 [Raven-Hart, *CGH* 2:432]

They are, without doubt, both in body and mind, the laziest people under the sun. . . . Their whole earthly happiness seems to lie in indolence and supinity.—Peter Kolb, 1719 [Kolb 1:46]

The men . . . are . . . the laziest creatures that can be imagined, since their custom is to do nothing, or very little. . . . If there is anything to be done, they let their women do it.—Francois Valentijn, 1726 [Valentijn 71–73]

[A] dull, inactive, and I had almost said, entirely listless disposition . . . is the leading characteristic of their minds . . . , necessarily produced by the debilitating diet they use, and their extreme inactivity and sloth.—Anders Sparrman, 1783 [Sparrman 209]

Lazy, idle, improvident. . . . —O. F. Mentzel, 1787 [Mentzel 2:276]

Perhaps the laziest nation upon earth. . . . [However] the women are very industrious in household affairs.—C. F. Damberger, 1801 [Damberger 57–58]

Though there are occasional dissenting voices,[2] and though the judgments of many writers are based on secondhand evidence or *idées reçues,* one must be struck by the persistence of these strictures, which continue into the period of British occupation of the Cape (see below). Idleness, indolence, sloth, laziness, torpor—these terms are meant both to define a Hottentot vice and to distance the writer from it. Nowhere in the great echo chamber of the Discourse of the Cape is a voice raised to ask whether the life of the Hottentot may not be a version of life before the Fall (as Bartolomé de las Casas suggested in respect of the Indians of the New World), a life in which man is not yet condemned to eat his bread in the sweat of his brow, but instead may spend his days dozing in the sun, or in the shade when the sun grows too hot, half-aware of the singing of the birds and the breeze on his skin, bestirring himself to eat when hunger overtakes him, enjoying a pipe of tobacco when it is available, at one with his surroundings and unreflectively content. The idea that the Hottentot may be Adam is not even entertained for the sake of being dismissed (on the grounds, say, that the Hottentot does not know God). Certainly no one dreams of asking whether what looks like Hottentot *dolce far niente* may not be the mere outward aspect of a profound Hottentot contemplative life. At a more practical level, no one asks for what reason a people whose traditional diet is meat, milk, and *veldkos* (forage food) should after 1652 decide that vegetables are better and begin to till the soil; or why, after artificial appetites for baked bread, tobacco, and spir-

2. See, for example, Grevenbroek, 1695, in Schapera 271–73.

its have been awoken in them, they should want to sell any more of their labour than would be required for the immediate satisfaction of these appetites. No one bothers to put, save rhetorically, the ethical question: which is better, to live like the ant, busily storing up food for winter, or like the grasshopper, singing in the sun all day, heedless of the morrow? The pastoral platitude that the wandering shepherd, with his meagre possessions and his easily satisfied wants, shows us a way of escaping from the cares of civilization, is nowhere spoken.

It is not enough to answer the question of why questions like these were not asked, by saying that the kind of person responsible for the Discourse of the Cape would never have thought of asking them. Certainly many of the travel writers were straightforward Company officials, ships' captains, or military men; but there were also scientists of distinction among them (Kolb, Sparrman), as well as men of learning (Ten Rhyne) and serious amateur observers (Schreyer). Furthermore, in Europe the fabled Hottentot did in time become a term in learned discourse, though less in inquiries into the natural state of man than in debate about whether there was a single creature called Man or several races of men, some nearer to beasts than others.[3] To understand why the Hottentot way of life, characterized by (and stigmatized for) its idleness, was in no way held up to Europe as a model of life in Eden, we must be aware of attitudes towards idleness prevailing in Europe at the time when Europe, and particularly Protestant Europe, was colonizing the Cape.

In the medieval Church contemplation was esteemed a higher kind of activity than work. The privileged position of the contemplative life was rejected by Luther as part of his rejection of a privileged spiritual status for the clergy. In Germany after the

---

3. François Bernier (1620–88) concludes that the Hottentots are "a different species" from the Negroes of Africa. John Locke (1632–1704), however, suggests that the intellect of the Hottentot seems "brutish" only because of environmental influences on him. Buffon (1707–88) contends that the distance between the Hottentot and the ape is far greater than the distance between the Hottentot and the rest of mankind. Johann Blumenbach (1752–1840) argues that, while the Hottentot may seem to belong to "a different species," there is in fact only "one variety of mankind." See Slotkin 95, 173, 184, 189.

Reformation in particular, preachers placed increasing emphasis on work as the fundamental divine edict, an edict that all men must obey to atone for Adam's fall. To be idle was to defy the edict; to be improvident—to depend on God's providence to save one from starving—was an aggravating offence, a provocative tempting of God. The devotional books of the period thunder against the "curse of idleness"; the community of Herrnhut, founded in 1727 and destined to form the model for the missions of the Moravian Brethren to the Hottentots of Africa, is representative of the age in writing into its statutes the requirement that everyone who joined the community had to labour for his own bread (Vontobel 67–70, 38; Marais 147–48).

As part of the Reformation, too, the Renaissance (and ultimately classical) distinction between base idleness and *otium*, time for self-cultivation, was rejected. Mankind was widely held to be so weak that without the discipline of continual work it was bound to relapse into sin. Bucer went so far as to suggest excommunication as the ultimate penalty for idleness (Vontobel 78). In Calvinism in particular, writes Max Weber, "waste of time [becomes] . . . the first and in principle the deadliest of sins. The span of human life is infinitely short and precious to make sure of one's own election. Loss of time through sociability, idle talk, luxury, even more sleep than is necessary for health . . . is worthy of absolute moral condemnation" (157–58).

At the same time a war on social parasitism was set in train. Even almsgiving was condemned as "a great sin" in that it encouraged people to evade God's edict on work (Vontobel 75). By the middle of the seventeenth century what Michel Foucault calls "the great confinement" had got under way. The culmination of a series of measures designed to put an end to vagrancy and begging as a way of life, it began with the confinement of the beggar class and went on later to sweep up the insane and the criminal. During crises of unemployment the houses of confinement became in effect prisons for the workless; during economic upswings they acted as hostels cum factories. As productive organizations these were a failure, but that did not matter: their purpose was not to turn a profit but to proclaim the ethical value of work. In this earliest phase of industrialization and this primitive phase of economic thinking, Foucault suggests, labour and poverty were held up as simple polar opposites: labour was imag- ined as having the power to abolish or overcome poverty "not so much by its productive capacity as by a certain force of moral enchantment" (*Madness and Civilization* 48–55).

Though conducted with greater ferocity in Protestant coun- tries, the war on beggars took place in both Catholic and Protes- tant Europe and continued as long as vagrancy remained a signifi- cant social problem, that is, well into the nineteenth century. The anathema on idleness, which was part of this war, did not falter with the Enlightenment; for the Enlightenment simply replaced the old condemnation of idleness as disobedience to God with an emphasis on work as a duty owed by man to himself and his neighbour. Through work man embarks on a voyage of explora- tion whose ultimate goal is the discovery of man; through work man becomes master of the world; through a community of work society comes into being. Karl Marx is wholly a child of the Enlight- enment when he writes, "The entire so-called history of the world is nothing but the creation of man through human labour" (305).

Both of the above attitudes—that idleness is a sin, that idleness is a betrayal of one's humanity—can be seen in the Discourse of the Cape. In the first hundred years or so of settlement, the idleness of the Hottentots is denounced in much the same spirit as the idleness of beggars and wastrels is denounced in Europe. One might say that the rhetoric used to justify class warfare in Europe is transferred wholesale and unthinkingly to the colony to condemn the refusal of the natives to be drawn into its econ- omy as wage labourers. This formulation must be qualified, how- ever. For the first wave of denunciation of Hottentot idleness belongs not so much to the discourse of the rulers of the Cape, where one might expect to find it if the problem of finding labour were uppermost, as to the rudimentary ethnographic dis- course of travel literature.[4] Furthermore, if one is to be drily

4. Van Riebeeck alludes to the idleness of the Hottentots only once, in a dispatch to the Chamber dated 14 April 1653, in which he begs to be removed from among these "dull, stupid, lazy, stinking people" to Japan, where his talents may be of more use. His *Journals* contain no reference to Hottentot idleness. Though his successors, Wagenaar and Borghorst, have more than a little to say about idleness, it is the idleness of the free farmers they condemn. See Van Riebeeck; D. Moodie 32, 270, 294, 304.

logical, sloth is precisely what the newly arrived colonizer might expect in a heathen folk who have not heard God's word and know nothing of the ban on idleness. In fact, the disguising of an attack on what we may call Hottentot passive resistance to wage-labour as a denunciation of idleness belongs to a later stage in the history of the Cape; the emphasis on Hottentot idleness in the literature, though understandable in observers with seventeenth-century Protestant backgrounds, is a response to more immediate frustrations. What the idleness of the Hottentot means to the early ethnographer becomes clear if we ask what it is that the Hottentot is *not doing* when he is found to be idle.

The charge of idleness often comes together with, and sometimes as the climax of, a set of other characterizations: that the Hottentots are ugly, that they never wash but on the contrary smear themselves with animal fat, that their food is unclean, that their meat is barely cooked, that they wear skins, that they live in the meanest of huts, that male and female mix indiscriminately, that their speech is not like that of human beings. What is common to these charges is that they mark the Hottentot as *underdeveloped*—underdeveloped not only by the standard of the European but by the standard of Man. If he were to develop dietary taboos, ablutionary habits, sexual mores, crafts, a more varied body decoration than uniform coating, domestic architecture and technology, a language of human articulations rather than animal noises, he would become, if not a Hollander, at least more fully Man. And the fact that he self-evidently does not employ his faculties in developing himself in these ways, but instead lies about in the sun, is proof that it is sloth that must be held accountable for retarding him.

What kind of creature is this Man whom the Hottentot, in his present state "to be counted more among the dumb beasts than among the company of reasoning men" (J. C. Hoffman, 1680 [L'Honoré Naber 31]), refuses out of idleness to become? It is Man with a developed Physical appearance, Dress, Diet, Medicine, Crafts, etc.—in other words, what we may call Anthropological Man. The Hottentot is Man but not yet Anthropological Man; and what keeps him in his backward state is idleness. Thus his idleness has the status of an anthropological scandal: despite the fact that nothing remoter and more different from European Man can be imagined than the Hottentot, the Hottentot, on closer inspection, turns out to yield an extremely impoverished set of differences to inscribe in the table of categories. Where he ought to be generating data for the categories, he is merely lying about. Where he ought to have Religion, there is a virtual blank. His Customs are casual. His Government is rudimentary. Though far more different from the European than the Turk or the Chinese is, the Hottentot paradoxically presents far fewer differences for the record.

The force of the righteous condemnation that the Discourse of the Cape brings to bear on the Hottentot comes from the accumulated weight of two centuries of denunciation of idleness, from the pulpit and the judicial bench, in Europe. But his idleness is responded to with particular animosity by the travel writer, the protoanthropologist, to whom he promises so much in the way of difference and yields so little. It is striking that, once we move out of the categorical discourse of anthropology, where the scheme requires the writer to inscribe eighteen or nineteen blocks with lists of remarkable differences, to the discourse of history, which at its simplest requires the writer merely to chronicle each day the remarkable events of that day, there is far less stress on the idleness of the Hottentots (see note 5, below). Indeed, in history the Hottentots suddenly seem all too busy, intriguing with one another, driving off cattle, begging, spying.

I am far from wanting to deny that, to the extent that the word *idle* has any objective meaning, the Hottentots were idle, or to assert that the condemnation of Hottentot idleness had nothing to do with the desire of the colonists to impress them as labourers. What I do wish to stress, however, is that the almost universal denunciation among the travel writers represents a reaction to a challenge, a scandal, that strikes particularly near to them *as writers;* that the laziness of the Hottentot aborts one of the more promising of discourses about elemental man. Nor is this generation of writers the last to respond with frustration to the recalcitrance of the colonies to generate materials to fill out its discourse. The ethnographer Gustav Fritsch, travelling around South Africa in the 1860s, observes that it would not be possible to use Boer life as material for stories because in Boer life nothing ever happens (161); and, at much the same time, Nathaniel Hawthorne is lamenting the "commonplace prosperity" without surprises and reversals, the "broad and simple daylight" of America, that make an American novel impossible (vi). In each case the colonial material is condemned as too exiguous for the European form; in each case the question is whether the new materials do not require a rethinking of old forms, old conceptual frameworks. The moment when the travel writer condemns the Hottentot for doing nothing is the moment when the Hottentot brings him face to face (if he will only recognize it) with his own preconceptions.

That this is a phenomenon of more significance than the failure of a set of casual writers with rough, workaday minds to escape their ethnocentric prejudices, can be seen from a landmark of anthropological writing, Jean-Jacques Rousseau's *Discourse on the Origin of Inequality* (1754). In a paragraph in which he specifically mentions the Hottentots, Rousseau characterizes Man in his savage state as "solitary, indolent [*oisif*], and perpetually accompanied by danger," a creature who "cannot but be fond of sleep." Man is lifted out of primitive savagery by the invention of tools, which bring about the first revolution in human culture and permit him an easier, less perilous life. In the new phase of comparative leisure [*loisir*] that tools permit, he begins to create conveniences for himself, conveniences which eventually develop into the yoke of civilization. The phase of leisure intermediate between savage indolence and the cultural revolution that will arrive with the invention of metallurgy and agriculture, the introduction of private property, the rise of social inequality, and the growth of work into an unavoidable part of daily life, is singled out by Rousseau as "the happiest and most stable of epochs. . . . The example of savages, most of whom have been found in this state, seems to prove that men were meant to remain in it, that it is the real youth of the world, and that all subsequent advances have . . . in reality [been steps] towards the decrepitude of the species" (169, 195–99).

When Rousseau comes to spell out what life might be like in this "happiest and most stable of epochs," the description he gives, though based on reports from the New World, could very well be a panorama of Hottentot life: people have rustic huts, clothes made of skins, adornments of feathers and shells, bows and arrows as weapons, clumsy musical instruments. What, then, is the crucial difference that prevents the Hottentot from being admitted to the golden age? Certainly his unsavoury personal habits and his infringement of European taboos on the preparation and consumption of meat play their part. But the essential difference is that the Hottentot is indolent, spending his "free" time sleeping, while among other savages who have passed through the toolmaking revolution free time becomes leisure, time devoted "industriously" to the elaboration of "conveniences" (ibid.). Rousseau thus, in line with Enlightenment thought, resurrects the humanistic opposition of leisure (Roman *otium*, Greek *schole*, time for self-improvement) to idleness: the Hottentot does not belong to the happiest of epochs because he is idle.[5] Leisure holds the promise of the generation of all those differences that constitute culture and make man Anthropological Man; idleness holds no promise save that of stasis.

II

Condemning the Hottentot for his idleness, the early Discourse of the Cape effectively excludes him from Eden by deciding that, though he is human, he is not in the line of descent that leads from Adam via a life of toil to civilized man. The Hottentot, that is to say, is not an original of civilized man. Although one cannot postulate that so farsighted an intention lay behind the strictures of the early writers, this conclusion nevertheless prepares the ground for the next phase of the attack on the Hottentot way of life, a way of life that, even as early as the mid-eighteenth century, was no longer confined to ethnic Hottentots but had found converts among Dutch Boers of the remoter frontiers. Thus O. F. Mentzel, who spent the years 1732–41 at the Cape, writes that some of these Boers "have accustomed themselves to such an extent to the carefree life,

5. On the classical background to the notion of leisure, see De Grazia 11–25.

the indifference, the lazy days and the association with slaves and Hottentots, that not much difference may be discerned between the former and the latter" (2:115). This "Hottentot" life of idleness and improvidence, this *lekker lewe*, never wins a spokesman in the Discourse of the Cape. The stratagem it might conceivably have resorted to—that of asserting an analogy between the Hottentot and unfallen man, between the Cape and Eden, and via this analogy claiming a tenuous legitimacy—is never used;[6] and though the idle life continues to be lived on all sides, it does so illegitimately, defensively, and invariably, when disclosed in print, as a scandal.

The indolence of the Hottentots is discovered afresh by British commentators after Britain's takeover of the Cape in 1795. Robert Percival writes of "the peculiar indolence and want of vigour of the Hottentot character," which he diagnoses as "an original bad quality" (84–85). John Barrow writes of indolence as "the principal cause of [the] ruin" of the Hottentots, "a real disease, whose only remedy seems to be that of terror," the remedy of hunger having shown itself to be inadequate (1:102). William Burchell praises the Moravian missionaries for their insistence on manual labour and predicts that once they have taught the Hottentots "the necessity of honest industry" they will have "cut off the root of, at least, half the miseries of the Hottentot race" (1:80). The consensus is that the Hottentot way of life, characterized by low-level subsistence maintained by the minimal resort to wage-labour ("laziness"), wandering in search of greener pastures ("vagrancy"), and a sometimes casual attitude toward private property ("thieving"), will have to be re-formed by *discipline* (a key word of the age) if the Hottentot is to have any stake ("pull his weight") in the Colony.

To the extent that it recognizes the fact that a Hottentot tribal life within the areas settled by colonists no longer exists and that the only viable future for the Hottentots is within the colonial economy, this attitude can be regarded as hardheaded. But to

6. For one exception to all the head-shaking, see Simon de la Loubiére, 1687: "In such poverty [the Hottentots] are always gay, always dancing and singing, living without occupation or toil" (Raven-Hart, *CGH* 2:269).

the extent that it sees "indolence" as part of the Hottentot racial "character," an "original bad quality" which only generations of strict discipline will eradicate ("cut off the root of"), we can accurately call it a racist attitude. It looks on the Hottentot and sees only squalor, disease, and blank torpor, closing its eyes to the possibility that, given a choice between idleness (with accompanying poverty) and the wretchedness of lifelong manual labour, people may deliberately choose the former. In contrasting inherent European diligence with inherent Hottentot sloth, it seems to forget the history of the early phase of industrialization in Europe, where it required a reformation of "character" occupying generations before the labouring class would embrace the principle that one should work harder than is required to maintain the level of material existence one is born into.[7] To bring about this reformation, to make people believe that "the opportunity of earning more was [more] attractive than that of working less," required a sustained programme of ideological indoctrination conducted through schools, churches, and the popular press, a programme meant to convince the lower classes that work was "necessary and noble" (Anthony 41, 22). A writer like Barrow, son of a self-made man and an influential adviser on colonial policy, is wholly committed to this ideology, as were the missionaries to whom the conduct of the programme of indoctrination was entrusted in the Colony. To persuade the Hottentots of Bethelsdorp to spend their time collecting the juice of aloes, John Philip of the London Missionary Society (LMS) allowed a shop to be opened on the mission station. The "experiment" of getting the Hottentots to work by holding before them the temptation of desirable articles for purchase succeeded: "Money instantly rose in estimation among them." The morality of what Philip admits to be "the creation of artificial wants" is irrelevant here. To Philip as a social thinker, the Hottentot clearly had no

7. Weber: "A man does not 'by nature' wish to earn more and more money, but simply to live as he is accustomed to live and to earn as much as is necessary for that purpose. Wherever modern capitalism has begun its work of increasing the productivity of human labour by increasing its intensity, it has encountered the immensely stubborn resistance of this leading trait of pre-capitalistic labour" (60). See also Hutt, chap. 5, "Preferred Idleness."

future unless he learned to sell his labour. As he candidly put it to his charges, they should not expect to use the mission stations as refuges from the dragnet of colonial authorities trying to tie them down as serfs on farms, as havens where a precolonial regime of idleness, improvidence, and easy morals might be maintained: quite aside from the fact that the missionaries would not sanction such a way of life, "the world, and the Church of Christ," which funded the missions, "looked for civilization and industry as proofs of [the Hottentots'] capacity for improvement . . . [since] men of the world had not other criteria by which they could judge" (1:204–05, ix, 212). In other words, if the Hottentots did not learn to work on the mission stations, the mission stations would close and they would be left to the mercies of the farmers. One way or the other, work they must. Thus, at the very time when the colonists were denouncing the LMS stations as "nests of idleness," idleness was what the missionaries saw as the one feature above all to be eradicated from the Hottentot "character."[8] If the LMS stations never became quite the hives of industry that the Moravian stations were reputed to be, it was largely because they did not practise the exclusion of people who came not to work but to share in the prosperity of their kinsfolk. As one observer lamented, the more industrious Hottentots of the Kat River settlement were having their wealth eaten up by "squatters" (presumably relatives) who "indulged in habitual sloth and listless inactivity"; and John Philip had similar criticisms to make of mission stations where "the means of the industrious [are] eaten up by the idle" (Marais 225, 249).

But the true scandal of the nineteenth century was not the idleness of the Hottentots (by now seen as inherent in the race) but the idleness of the Boers. The sliding of farmers into an idle way of life can be traced back to the first decades of settlement. Governor Wagenaar, Van Riebeeck's successor, wrote to

8. "Nests of idleness" is the phrase used by the colonial magistrates in 1849 in their denunciation of the mission stations (Marais 197). For the comments of Rev. John Campbell, inspector of the LMS stations, on the "idleness and sloth" of Hottentots who come to the stations from both kraals and farms, see Campbell 92–93. See also Burchell's report that the missionaries at Klaarwater continually complained of "the laziness of the Hottentots" (1:246).

the Chamber in 1663 suggesting that half a dozen of the free farmers ought to be called home because of their "indolence and . . . irregular and debauched lives." From the Chamber, familiar with the problem from the Indies, he received a tolerant reminder that "our people, when abroad, are at all times with difficulty induced to work," and the suggestion that he should rely more on slaves (D. Moodie 270, 279). "Too much good fortune hath bred sloth among the farmers," writes Grevenbroek in 1695 (Schapera 273). A century later Le Vaillant comments that "from the profound inaction in which they live, one would suppose their supreme felicity to consist in doing nothing."[9]

Not only the farmer but the burgher of Cape Town was afflicted with this lapse into sloth. Stavorinus describes a typical day in the life of a burgher at the end of the eighteenth century: a long smoke and stroll in the morning, an hour or two of business, a midday meal followed by a snooze, an evening of cards—all in all "a very comfortable life" (248). Percival and Barrow confirm his account a decade later: "A most lamentable picture of laziness and indolent stupidity," Percival calls it (Percival 255; Barrow 2:100–01).

The harshest remarks of nineteenth-century commentators are, however, reserved for the Boers of the frontier. In his survey of the productive potential of the Colony, Barrow writes, "Luckily, perhaps, for them, the paucity of ideas prevents time from hanging heavy on their hands. . . . [Theirs is a] cold phlegmatic temper and [an] inactive way of life . . . , indolence of body and a low groveling mind." Seeing sloth as by now part of the "nature" of the Boer, Barrow suggests that the Colony will not become productive until this "nature" is changed, or, failing that, until the Boers are replaced with more industrious and enterprising settlers (1:32; 2:118; 1:386).

The refrain is taken up by every traveller who penetrates into the back country and encounters farmers living in mean dwellings set on vast tracts, barely literate, rudely clad, surrounded by slaves and servants with too little employment, disdainful of man-

9. Le Vaillant 1:59. See also Paterson 84.

ual labour, content to carry on subsistence farming in a land of potential plenty. Percival comments, "There is I believe in no part of the world an instance to be found of European adventurers so entirely destitute of enterprise, and so completely indifferent to the art of bettering their situation." The women of the frontier he finds particularly "lazy, listless and inactive," a judgment confirmed by J. W. D. Moodie: they are "exceedingly torpid and phlegmatic in their manners and habits, dirty and slovenly in their dress" (Percival 211; Moodie 1:170). On the frontier "days and years pass in miserable idleness," says John Campbell (81). Burchell observes that the new immigrant, full of enterprise and energy, swiftly rises to prosperity, but then "adopts the rude manners [of the Africander] he at first despised, and, step by step, his life degenerates into mere sensual existence." Burchell repeats Barrow's diagnosis that sloth has become part of the Boer character, and follows Barrow's prescription that some kind of missionary work will be necessary to bring the Boer into the modern world: "The ease of an indolent life, with all its losses, is so much more agreeable to [them] than the labour of an industrious one with all its advantages, that the lives of such men must be entirely new-modelled before they can be capable of receiving the improvements of other countries" (1:194, 377). Fifty years after Burchell, Gustav Fritsch finds among the Boers "a degree of indolence and indifference [that is] absolutely Chinese in its constancy" (89–90); and the Carnegie Commission of the 1930s notes again the "indolence" of the "poor white" descendants of these farmers, an indolence which it ascribes to, inter alia, the South African climate, prejudice against "kaffir work," and a tradition of easy existence (Wilcocks 52–79).

The spokesmen of colonialism are dismayed by the squalor and sloth of Boer life because it affords sinister evidence of how European stock can regress after a few generations in Africa.[10]

10. Degeneracy was already held in prospect by Mentzel in 1787. Writing of those Boers who "prefer to live in the most distant wilderness among the Hottentots," he expresses his fear that if they do not intermarry with new European stock they will "degenerate and become uncivilized," like the Scots or Wends or Scythians: already "their nature is wild, their education bad, their thoughts base and their conduct ill-bred" (2:120).

In being content to scratch no more than a bare living from the soil, the Boer seems further to betray the colonizing mission, since in order to justify its conquests colonialism has to demonstrate that the colonist is a better steward of the earth than the native (the text usually cited in support is Matthew 25 : 14–30, the parable of the talents). Nor can one neglect the element of chauvinism in the comparison British commentators draw between the diligent English yeoman and the listless Dutch boer.

But there is a further component to the British response to Boer idleness, a component of moral outrage stemming from the perception that Boer ease is achieved at the expense of the misery of slaves and servants. The ease of the farmers is scandalous because it is corrupt: the case of the Cape Colony seems to confirm the dictum going back to antiquity (see Davis chap. 3; Lecky 1:277) that slaveholding corrupts the slaveholder. "The possession of slaves, and the subjection of the Hottentots . . . have been the source of the greatest demoralization of all classes in this colony" (J. W. D. Moodie 1:176). "The taint of slavery, here as elsewhere makes the white man lazy" (Alexander 1:70). In the Cape the taint works in a particularly insidious way because, aside from the slaveowner's own prejudice against manual labour, idleness as a pervasive way of life also has the consequence that about each farmer-patron there comes to cluster a band of dependants and hangers-on doing little work and getting the poorest of wages. Thus while disdain for work becomes institutionalized among the masters, the system does not even have the compensation that habits of industry are fostered among the servants—who are frequently found to prefer Boer masters to British because the latter, though they pay more, demand too much work (Marais 130–31).

On the other hand, the idleness of the Boers does not create the same crisis for the commentator *as writer* that the idleness of the Hottentot created in the seventeenth century. For while the framework of the earlier writing was that of a nascent science of Man, with universal and therefore obligatory cultural categories, nineteenth-century commentary takes the form of episodic narrative in which the narrator is free to move across the face of the Colony, seeing sights, having hunting adventures, meeting new people, recording anecdotes and oddities. The genre is, in fact, *causerie*, as the typically extended chapter headings indicate.[11] In this mode almost any material is fit to fill the ethnographic space left by Hottentot and Boer inactivity, as long as it is diverting.

The fact that Boer idleness is achieved at the expense of a servile class and therefore differs in a crucial respect from the old Hottentot idleness has the natural consequence that the philosophical question that did not get asked regarding the Hottentots gets asked all the less regarding the Boers, namely, if we ignore the dirty skins, the clouds of flies, the rude clothing can these frontier farmers not be said to stand for a rejection of the curse of discipline and labour in favour of a prelapsarian African way of life in which the fruits of the earth are enjoyed as they drop into the hand, work is avoided as a scourge, and idleness and leisure become the same thing? The moral and political outlook of the typical British visitor to the Cape made it unlikely that such a thought would be entertained. Nevertheless, the fantasy of an African Eden does not get suppressed entirely, particularly once the efforts of the first wave of literary Romanticism to locate unfallen man in the child or the peasant or the savage have made the quest for man's origins a commonplace of travel writing. Certainly no one asks whether the torpor of the Hottentot or the sloth of the Boer is a sign that all wants have been met, all desires have been stilled, and Eden has been recovered. But there is a revealing moment in the *Travels* of Burchell, perhaps of nineteenth-century commentators the most readily sympathetic to native ways of life. In 1812 Burchell spent an evening among a group of Bushmen somewhere between Prieska and De Aar noting down their music and watching their dancing. At midnight he retired to bed. Of the evening he says:

> Had I never seen and known more of these savages than the occurrences of this day, and the pastimes of this evening, I should not have hesitated to declare them the happiest of mor-

11. A typical chapter summary: "Wesleyville—Its delightful scenery—Second and third missionary stations—Interpreters and guides—Anecdotes of the elephants—Strange scenes—Hottentot eloquence—Grave argument—Artifice—Criticism, and humour—Games—Evening amusements—Shooting hippopotami—The River Kei—The Incagalo—Kaffir chief and his staff—Anecdotes" (Rose x).

tals. Free from care, and pleased with little, their life seemed flowing on, like a smooth stream gliding through flowery meads. Thoughtless and unreflecting, they laughed and smiled the hours away, heedless of futurity, and forgetful of the past.

Though hedged around with conditions ("Had I never seen and known more . . . "), this is a vision of man before the Fall, a vision whose seductions Burchell acknowledges: "I sat as if the hut had been my home, and felt in the midst of this horde as if I had been one of them; for some moments . . . forgetting that I was a lonely stranger in a land of wild untutored men" (2:48). Even Barrow, so censorious of the Boers, so dismissive of the Hottentots ("perhaps the most wretched of the human race" [1:93]), can be impressed by the Kaffirs and speculate that their natural nobility of bearing must be the consequence of simple diet, regular habits, abstinence from alcohol, pure air, plenty of exercise, and physical chastity— in other words, the consequence of freedom from the more debilitating features of civilization, in a regime which the British public school would later try to reproduce. But what draws Barrow to these African Spartans is in the first place their "sprightliness, activity and vivacity" (1:119), while Burchell's eulogy comes only after the Bushmen have danced "till morning light announced that other duties claimed their time." It would seem that the savage has to bend his neck to the yoke of "activity," "duties," before the thought may be admitted that he belongs to the Golden Age.

III

Today we are not likely to be so censorious of the idleness of the Hottentots (the Boers present a somewhat different case). We have a century of anthropological and historical discipline behind us to make us wary of observing the lives of foreign peoples too cursorily and from too self-centred a viewpoint. Given a chance to visit the seventeenth-century Cape, we might reasonably expect to see features of Hottentot life that eluded seventeenth-century observers. We might be more sensitive to seasonal variations in activity and to the rhythm of the Hottentot "week." We might be more hesitant about calling an entire people lazy on the grounds that the men lie around while the women are busy (a fact that several early travellers noted). We might pay less attention to hunting and fishing and ways of dressing flesh—an area where taboos tend to clash—and more to the gathering activities of women and children. We might be more cautious of taking those Hottentots on the fringes of Dutch settlement as typical of all Hottentots.[12] With our wider historical perspective, we might also appreciate better what a massive cultural revolution is entailed when a people moves from a subsistence economy to an economy of providence, from pastoralism to agriculture—a move, indeed, in which the notion of *work* may be said to make its appearance in history.

Yet in the very openmindedness we might like to imagine extending toward the Hottentot from our modern science of Man lies the germ of an insidious betrayal of the Hottentot. For, no less than in the science of Man that met and was frustrated by the real Hottentots, the modern science of Man has at its foundation a will to see a culture at work in a society. The science of Man is itself a discipline, one of what Foucault calls the disciplines of surveillance; among its tasks are the tracking down and investigating of obscure societies in all quarters of the globe, the photographing and recording and deciphering of their activities (*Discipline and Punish* 224). If the Hottentot did not absorb the ideology of work in a generation, we cannot expect the Western bourgeois to shed his allegiance to it in a day. It would be particularly rash to expect that the modern researcher and writer would respond more generously than his ancestors to a way of life so indolent that, in its extreme form, it presented him with nothing to say. The temptation to say that there is something *at work* when there is nothing is always strong. The present chapter does not entirely resist that temptation. The challenge of idleness to work, its power to scandalize, is as radical today as it ever was. Indeed—though it takes us outside the bounds of the present discussion—we might wonder whether the challenge presented

12. Marshall Sahlins describes "the characteristic paleolithic rhythm of a day or two on, a day or two off" (23). Richard B. Lee, writing of the Dobe Bushmen, hunter-gatherers, observes how surprisingly high a proportion of their food intake comes from vegetable foods collected by women (33). Richard Elphick discusses the effect of "radically foreign" customs on the formation of European prejudice against the Hottentots (193–200).

by idleness to the philosophical enterprise is any less powerful or subversive than the challenge presented by the erotic, in particular by the *silence* of eroticism (see Bataille 273–76).

The history of idleness in South Africa is not a side issue or a curiosity. One need only look at the face of South African labour in the twentieth century to confirm this. The idleness of the Boer is still there in taboos on certain grades of manual work (*hotnotswerk, kafferwerk*), as well as in rituals of leisure indistinguishable from idleness (sitting on the porch, lying on the beach). The idleness of the native is still present in a tradition of overemployment and underpayment, maintained from both sides of the fence, in terms of which two men are hired to do one man's work, each working half the time and standing idle half the time, each getting half of one man's wage. The luxurious idleness of the settler is still denounced from Europe, the idleness of the native still deplored by his master. I hope that it is clear that I by no means add my voice to the chorus of moralizing disapproval. On the contrary, I hope that I have opened a way to the reading of idleness since 1652 as an authentically native response to a foreign way of life, a response that has rarely been defended in writing, and then only evasively (one thinks of H. C. Bosman), but that has exerted a powerful popular attraction since the days when commentators began to shake their heads over Europeans who, from too much intercourse with Hottentots, were sinking into a life of sloth. It is a measure of how powerful this attraction has remained into our times that, after 1948, the authorities embarked—and, to the extent that they were responding to social realities, found themselves compelled to embark—on a programme of laws to re-form South African society. Two cornerstone measures of this programme were the so-called Immorality Act and Mixed Marriages Act, laws whose primary intention and whose practical effect it was to take away from white men the freedom to drop out of the ranks of the labouring class, take up with brown women, settle down to more or less idle, shiftless, improvident lives, and engender troops of ragged children of all hues, a process which, if allowed to accelerate, would in the end, they foresaw, spell the demise of White Christian civilisation at the tip of Africa.

2

The Picturesque, the Sublime,
and the South African Landscape

William Burchell

Between 1811 and 1813 William Burchell, botanist, ornithologist, anthropologist, natural historian, travelled some forty-five hundred miles across the Cape Colony and beyond its borders. In his *Travels in the Interior of Southern Africa* (1822) Burchell left a comprehensive account of his researches in the vast and sparsely settled hinterland of Britain's new colony.

Besides being a man of science, Burchell was an accomplished amateur painter and a thoughtful observer of the South African landscape. Shortly after arriving at the Cape he was taken to see the view over what are now the National Botanic Gardens at Kirstenbosch. He comments,

> The view from this spot . . . is the most picturesque of any I had seen in the vicinity of Cape Town. The beauties here displayed to the eye could scarcely be represented by the most skilful pencil; for this landscape possessed a character that would require the combined talents of a Claude and a Both; but at this hour, the harmonious effect of light and shade, with the enchanting appearance of foliage in the foreground, and

the tone of the middle distances, were altogether far beyond the painter's art. The objects immediately surrounding us, were purely sylvan; a blue extent of distance terminated the landscape both in front and on the right. To the left, the noble Table Mountain rose in all its grandeur. . . . The last beams of the sun, gleaming over the rich, varied, and extensive prospect, laid on the warm finishing lights, in masterly and inimitable touches. [*Travels* 1:51–52]

Burchell records the Kirstenbosch scene only in words. But they are the words of an enthusiast of landscape, that is to say, of an observer who views terrain as a potential subject of painting, and whose observation of terrain is in turn educated by his experience of painting. (The word *landscape,* which we use today to designate both a specific terrain and the general character of that terrain, enters English in the sixteenth century as a term from the art of painting: landscapes were pictures of stretches of countryside.) Burchell's comments on the difficulties of rendering the tone, light, and chiaroscuro of Kirstenbosch are not empty exclamations but judicious aesthetic observations. Composing the scene in his paragraph as planes of foreground, middle ground, and far distance, with the mountain forming a *coulisse* on the left, he follows pictorial principles. His mention of "warm finishing lights" reveals the medium in which he projects the scene: oils. He even specifies the landscape tradition within which he is thinking: the tradition of Claude, particularly of Claude as seen through English eyes—that is, the tradition of the picturesque.

Once Burchell leaves Cape Town and passes the Hex River Mountains, however, he finds himself in terrain that does not readily lend itself to being picturesquely conceived. "A desolate, wild, and singular landscape," he writes on 9 September 1811. "The only colour we beheld was a sterile brown . . . ; nothing but rocks and stones lay scattered every where around." To evoke the picturesque in his sketches, he finds, he must incorporate into their foreground his caravan of wagons, oxen, and sheep (1:206); and without water, expanses of water, the scene still lacks life. Arrival at the Gariep River evokes the following effusion:

> The first view to which I happened to turn myself . . . realized
> those ideas of elegant and classic scenery, which are created in
> the minds of poets. . . . The waters of the majestic river, flow-
> ing in a broad expanse resembling a smooth translucent lake,
> seemed, with their gentle waves, to kiss the shore . . . , bearing
> on their limpid bosom the image of their wood-clothed
> banks. . . . Rapt with pleasing sensations which the scenery in-
> spired, I sat on the bank a long time contemplating the serenity
> and beauty of the view. [1:221–22]

His relief at discovering in this hot, alien land a scene that, if not
breathing domestic associations, at least does not resist the imposition of a familiar aesthetic schema is palpable.

In the second volume of the *Travels* Burchell returns several
times to the problem hinted at in the above passage: Are the
banks of the Gariep an oasis in the African aesthetic wilderness,
or is there an African species of beauty to which the eye nurtured on the European countryside, trained on European pictorial art, is blind? If the latter, is it possible for a European to
acquire an African eye? Contemplating a typical stretch of what
later writers will call "the veld," Burchell answers himself as follows:

> In the character of [this] *landscape* and its peculiar tints, a
> painter would find much to admire, though it differed entirely
> from the species known by the term 'picturesque.' But it was
> not the less beautiful: nor less deserving of being studied by
> the artist: it was that kind of *harmonious beauty* which belongs to
> the extensive plains of Southern Africa. The pale yellow dry
> grass gave the prevailing colour, and long streaks of bushes as
> it seemed, parallel to the horizon and gradually fading into the
> distance, sufficiently varied the uniformity of the plain; while
> clumps of the soft and elegant acacia, presented a feature
> which relieved these long streaks by an agreeable change of
> tint, and by the most pleasing forms backed by low azure hills
> in the farthest distance.

It requires the addition only of horses and oxen grazing in the
foreground, Burchell continues, to complete "a landscape, perhaps altogether inimitable . . . which, if put on canvas, would . . .
prove to European painters that there exists . . . a species of

beauty with which, possibly, they may not yet be sufficiently acquainted" (2:194).

In these and other passages, Burchell pleads on two grounds for aesthetic appreciation of the South African landscape. The first ground is that European standards of beauty are linked too closely to the picturesque, which is only one of several varieties of the beautiful. The second is that the European eye will be disappointed in Africa only as long as it seeks in African landscapes European tones and shades. I would like to examine these grounds more closely; but first we must be clear about what Burchell means by "the picturesque."

The practice among Englishmen of travelling for the purpose of viewing natural scenery may be said to begin after 1713, when the Treaty of Utrecht opened up the Continent to the so-called Grand Tour. In Rome, travellers on the Grand Tour made the acquaintance of Italian landscape art, particularly the paintings of Claude Lorraine and Salvator Rosa, and carried home a taste for them. Till at least the end of the century in England, and for another half-century at least in the colonies and ex-colonies, enthusiasm for painting in the style of Claude and Salvator, and consequently for natural scenes of the kind depicted in their paintings, all under the name *the picturesque,* remained a mark of a cultivated taste.

Landscape is picturesque when it composes itself, or is composed by the viewer, in receding planes according to the Claudian scheme: a dark *coulisse* on one side shadowing the foreground; a middle plane with a large central feature such as a clump of trees; a plane of luminous distance; perhaps an intermediate plane too between middle and far distance. Enthusiasm for landscape of this type was a powerful factor in determining the course both of English nature poetry (James Thomson, for instance, is clearly familiar with Claude) and of English landscape gardening. The picturesque, as defined by its great theorist Uvedale Price and popularized in the books of William Gilpin, for a while held in England a position of significance near to that of the beautiful and the sublime as an aesthetic category. The ideally picturesque view, Gilpin suggested, contained distant mountains, a lake in the middle distance, and a foreground of rocks, woods, broken ground, cascades, or ruins, this foreground to be characterized by "force and richness," by "roughness" of texture, in contrast to the "tenderness" of the middle and far ground (Clark 64; Noyes 11–17, 42; Barrell 21; Watson 31).

It is worth stressing that, as the word *landscape* is both topographical and aesthetic in its reference, the word *picturesque* refers to nature and art at the same time, that is, to physical landscape conceived of pictorially. In this respect, as Karl Kroeber points out, the picturesque differs from the beautiful and the sublime, which refer to either art or nature but not to a relation between the two (5).

In historical retrospect, we now recognize that the picturesque performed a transitional function, for the space of several decades bridging the gap between a waning neoclassicism—to be seen most clearly in Claude's literary landscapes, with their nostalgia for the world of Theocritus and Virgil—and the growing Romantic taste for variety of light and shade, abruptness, what Uvedale Price calls "intricacy" or surface variation (Watson 19–20). By 1800, the picturesque had ceased to be a living force in English aesthetic thought. Wordsworth speaks for this movement in taste when, looking back to his early enthusiasm for the picturesque, he criticizes himself for

> giving way
> To a comparison of scene with scene,
> [Being] bent overmuch on superficial things,
> Pampering myself with meagre novelties
> Of colour and proportion.
>
> [*Prelude* (1805) 11:157–61]

Yet the picturesque is more than a makeshift bridging movement in the history of sensibility. The cult of the picturesque made the contemplation of landscape a widespread cultural recreation. A generation learned not only to view terrain as a structure of natural elements with analyzable relations one to another, but to be aware of the associations, natural and acquired, borne by these elements. Picturesque landscape is, in effect, landscape reconstituted in the eye of the imagination according to acquired principles of composition. Wordsworth's own theory of the imagination responds to the question of how landscape can be composed as a significant whole in the imagination in the absence of some aesthetic principle, taken over from what he calls "the cold rules of painting," to give it unity.[1]

Though the picturesque had ceased to be a force in aesthetic debate by the time Burchell published his *Travels* in 1822, it remained a term in wide currency among educated people. Arguing for aesthetic appreciation of the landscape of the South African plateau, Burchell, as we have seen, takes the position that, though it may not be picturesque, this landscape possesses a certain "harmonious beauty" deserving of study. Such study, he implies, may yield a uniquely African aesthetic schema parallel to the Claudian schema of the picturesque, and this in turn may provide the basis for aesthetic satisfactions paralleling the aesthetic satisfactions afforded by European picturesque landscape.

The idea is potentially revolutionary. Yet as Burchell adumbrates what an African beauty might consist in, we recognize that it is but a modified European picturesque, particularly in the prominence it awards to the infinite perspective ("long streaks of bushes . . . gradually fading into the distance . . . low azure hills in the farthest distance"). We should recall that if one feature of Claude's paintings above all captured the imagination of the eighteenth century, it was the inimitable luminous, far-off glow into which the viewer's gaze was slowly but ineluctably absorbed. In recession into the infinite, Burchell asserts, Africa can match Europe; as regards the middle ground, Africa is varied enough, once the eye has accustomed itself to more subdued tonal values; while if the foreground tends to be empty, matter enough can be found with which to fill it. Plate I of the second volume of the *Travels* provides an example: Burchell fills the near ground with a bed of waving reeds and introduces his travelling companions

1. In a note to line 347 of the "Descriptive Sketches" of 1793, Wordsworth observes that he decided against the title "Picturesque Sketches" because the "cold rules of painting" (which he associates with the picturesque) can never express the feelings of someone confronted with the grandeur of the Alps (*Poetical Works* 1:62). Nevertheless, as mature a work as "Tintern Abbey" (written 1798) is scenically structured on the Claudian model.

receding from him in file; he even incorporates a *coulisse* in the shape of a shadowed, rocky hillside.

Less disappointing than his observations on composition are Burchell's remarks on colour and tone. He is continually on the lookout for green. Of the landscape of the Kareeberg he writes, "The only colour we beheld was a sterile brown, softening into azure or purple in the distance: the eye sought in vain for some tint of verdure" (1:206). On the banks of the Gariep "[The] lively yellow-green [of the willows] . . . had a cheerful effect on the spirits and relieved the eye by a hue most soothing and grateful" (1:222). In the Asbestos Mountains bushes "[enliven] with tints of verdure the rich and varied browns of [the] broken crags" (2:5). The paucity of greens, the subdued tone of what green does occur ("that broad and green foliage, that fresh and lively complexion [of England], do not belong to the general character of the woods and thickets of the interior"), combine with an overall thinness of hue: "In Africa we look in vain for those mellow beautiful tints with which the sun of autumn dyes the forests of England" (2:9). Even the African dawn is "[deficient in] those rosy and golden tints . . . which decorate the morning sky of European countries," the cause of this deficiency being the absence of cloud and vapour in the atmosphere (2:231).

It is not surprising that Burchell, as an Englishman writing for English readers, should continually point to differences between the landscapes of Africa and England. But his painterly terminology reminds us that he writes, as well, as an artist, and an artist brought up in the English landscape school. For such an artist, what problems does the African landscape present? The list might include the following. First, the artist's entire palette must be modified and subdued: deep greens being rare, the discrimination of shades of green at which north European landscape art excels must be replaced by discrimination of a variety of fawns, browns, and greys. Second, since foliage adapted to a dry climate transpires very little, it lacks lustre. Third, light tends to be bright and even, transitions from light to shade abrupt. Fourth, the reflective medium of surface water is rare, the diffusive medium of atmospheric moisture only slightly less so.

I have already discussed the debt of English picturesque art to the Italianate tradition, that is, to Italian Renaissance models as filtered through the work of Claude. This tradition was grafted, principally by Gainsborough, on to an English tradition that continued to find its subjects in local topography but learned much of its technique from the Dutch landscape school of Hobbema and Ruysdael (Paulson 47). If we seek reasons why English landscape art of Burchell's day should have found itself ill prepared for the African landscape, should even have found the African landscape intractable, we should look not only to the resistance of that landscape to being composed according to the picturesque schema, but to the predispositions of north European oil painting technique. I have mentioned the bias of the north European palette (and eye) toward rich greens and the general depth of tone of north European landscape art. But shade and water are equally important.

The great technical achievement of John Constable was to create means of rendering transitory effects of sunlight on surfaces—what he called "the evanescent effects of nature's chiaroscuro." There are two sides to the phrase "nature's chiaroscuro" as Constable uses it: first, the sparkle of light, particularly as reflected from objects touched with moisture (e.g., dew) or bursting with moist life, a sparkle that Constable rendered with touches of white from a palette knife; and second, the opposition and interplay of light and shade in landscape. "Remember light and shadow never stand still," he writes (Clark 75–76, 32).

Light and shadow never stand still for Ruysdael or Constable because, in Holland or England, there is always cloud movement in the sky. Over the southern African plateau, however, skies are blue, light and shadow are static (which is why writers repeatedly characterize the landscape as sleeping, torpid, heatstruck). Peculiarities of atmospheric conditions in northern Europe thus make for developments in European art that have no obvious relevance to southern Africa. When we broaden the discussion to take in the general dryness of South African conditions, as opposed to the moistness of English conditions, we come to touch on questions that are not merely technical but produce radical differences of material culture between two societies, even, one might speculate, radical differences of cultural outlook. It is no accident that the

Lake District became the destination par excellence for the picturesque tourist. By the aid of lakes, wrote Wordsworth in his *Guide
through the District of the Lakes*, "the imagination . . . is carried into
recesses of feeling otherwise impenetrable. The reason of this is,
that the heavens are not only brought down into the bosom of the
earth, but the earth is mainly looked at, and thought of, through
the medium of a purer element" (191–92).

Gilpin too found lakes rich in meaning: "These rich volumes of
nature, like the works of established authors, will bear a frequent
perusal" (Watson 47). Tranquil water is the only reflective medium in nature, by its nature a medium to tranquility and reflection. But, as Wordsworth points out, lake water is also transparent, its transparency rendering it penetrable into its depths by the
eye, the mind. Bodies of still water lend themselves to metaphors
of thinking; in European Romantic landscape art they are associated with reflection, contemplation, and the values attached to the
contemplative posture. In lakes and pools, like Narcissus, we see
ourselves, come to self-consciousness, for the first time. Surface
water—lakes, rivers, streams, pools—more than any other natural
feature except perhaps trees and mountain peaks becomes a locus
of meanings as well as an element of construction in landscape art.
What concerns us here is, by contrast, the near absence of surface
water on the South African plateau, and the consequent lacuna in
the repertoire of the artist (painter but also writer) wishing to give
meaningful (meaning-filled) representation to that landscape within the schema he has carried over from European art. In the rarity
of bodies of still water in South Africa, European-descended landscape writing finds confirmation, and perhaps even occasion, for
several of its commonest themes: that in South Africa the earth
and the heavens are separate and even sundered realms; that the
earth is dead or sleeping or insentient—in Thoreau's figure, lacks
an eye; that no dialogue can be carried on with it.[2]

2. "A lake is the landscape's most beautiful expressive feature. It is earth's
eye." Also: "While men believe in the infinite some ponds will be thought to be
bottomless." Thoreau 186, 287. The figure of the eye is repeated in Bachelard.
"A lake, a pool, still water—each makes us stop at its edge. It tells the will: you
shall not pass; you have to go back to looking at distant things, things beyond! . . .
A lake is a great tranquil eye" (77).

Thomas Pringle

Thomas Pringle (1789–1834), who spent six years in South Africa during the 1820s, is the only Romantic writer of any attainment to have visited the Colony. Pringle left behind a fair body of impressions of the South African landscape in verse and prose. Before turning to these, however, I would like to quote from "The Autumnal Excursion" of 1816, a poem that shows Pringle still closely wedded to eighteenth-century models of landscape verse, and in particular to the conventions of the picturesque. After establishing the appropriately meditative mood—

> I love the blithesome harvest morn,
> Where Ceres pours her plenteous horn . . .
> But yet, my friend, there is an hour . . .
> When the full heart, in pensive tone,
> Sighs for a scene more wild and lone—

he writes of the Tweedside where he grew up:

> Oft from yon height [Mount Blaiklaw] I loved to mark
> Soon as the morning roused the lark,
> And woodlands raised their raptured hymn,
> That land of glory spreading dim;
> While slowly up the awakening dale
> The mists withdrew their fleecy veil,
> And tower, and wood, and winding stream,
> Were brightening to the orient beam.
> —Yet where the westward shadows fell,
> My eye with fonder gaze would dwell; . . .
> There stood a simple home . . .
> A rustic dwelling, thatched and warm . . .
> And there the wall-spread apple-tree
> Gave its white blossoms to the bee,
> Beside the hop-bower's twisted shade
> Where age reclined and childhood played.
> Below, the silvery willows shook
> Their tresses o'er the rambling brook,
> That gambolled 'mong its banks of broom,
> Till lost in Lerdan's haunted gloom,
> Methinks I hear that streamlet's din
> Where straggling alders screen the linn,

> Gurgling into its fairy pool,
> With pebbled bottom clear and cool.[3]

In this poem we see both the enthusiasm for shade, solitude, and mouldering ruins and the careful scenic composition characteristic of picturesque art. Certainly it is the eye of childhood memory that beholds the Tweedside landscape; but this eye is first removed to a hilltop, from whose vantage the landscape is composed, item by item, as a *prospect* in the tradition of poems like Dyer's "Grongar Hill," before the picturesque composition is rendered in words. This rendering into words clearly takes into account procedures whereby painting is read, particularly the order in which the eye decodes the elements of a well-composed painting. Of course the picture in Pringle's eye is not composed with quite the care of the painter's art; nor, working in a linear medium, does he have the painter's planar resources; so what he follows in the writing is not quite the progress of the eye decoding the mental picture along lines of compositional structure, so much as a few of the movements of the eye standard to the reading of picturesque painting: for instance, the progress of the gaze up a mist-shrouded valley toward the horizon (rather than down the valley); or along the path of a stream from near ground till it loses itself.

The hilltop situation of the observing eye does more than create a prospect. It also, as John Barrell (21) points out, puts the kind of phenomenological distance between viewer and landscape that exists between viewer and painting, creating a predisposition to see landscape as art (the use of the Claude glass is the

---

3. Sources for poems cited hereafter are as follows: Peter Blum, "Nuus uit die binneland": Opperman 424; Roy Campbell, "An Anatomy of the Veld," "A Veld Eclogue: The Pioneers": Campbell 100–01, 113–16; H. H. Dugmore, "A South African Wilderness": Dugmore 73–75; William Hamilton, "The Song of an Exile": Butler & Mann 59; Uys Krige, "Verre blik": Opperman 206; W. E. G. Louw, "Adam": Opperman 223–27; S. Ignatius Mocke, "Die Vrystaat": Opperman 215; Thomas Pringle, "The Autumnal Excursion": *Poetical Works* 117–34; "Evening Rambles," "The Desolate Valley": *Poems Illustrative of South Africa* 20–26, 70–73; Ina Rousseau, "Eden": Opperman 409; F. D. Sinclair, "Christmas Night 1944": Sinclair 39; Francis Carey Slater, "The Karroo": Slater 201–13; C. M. van den Heever, "O verre wydtes": *Versamelde gedigte* 158.

logical and ultimate extension of hilltop practice, putting a frame around the prospect and toning down its colour). Furthermore, the hilltop explicitly defines the poet's position in space and therefore seems to renounce the freedom of the mind's (or memory's) eye, which can roam where it will, in favour of the painter's single viewpoint. Toward the end of the extract Pringle uses an uneasy device ("Methinks I hear . . .") to free himself from this single perspective. For the sake of what does he yield up the painter's position? To move to something "lost in Lerdan's haunted gloom," invisible from the hilltop, namely, the clear waters of a pool.

The most notable topographic poem Pringle wrote in South Africa is his "Evening Rambles." In the construction of this poem we again see the procedures of picturesque painting (and viewing) at work. It begins with a panorama that announces the contrast between settled valley (Pringle's Glen Lynden) and surrounding mountains:

> Soothing recollections fail
> [When] we raise the eye to range
> O'er prospects wild, grotesque, and strange;
> Sterile mountains, rough and steep,
> That bound abrupt the valley deep.

The disturbing panorama of the mountains is countered by a more reassuring progress of the eye up the valley into the "stream of light descending" in the distance, and then by several more traverses whose effect is to cover the whole space of the landscape. I will not discuss these traverses in detail, except to observe that they are accomplished with a fair amount of art. One traverse is dramatized as a walk by the poet through a "maze" of acacias during which a variety of bird and animal life presents itself to him; in another traverse his eye follows the course of darkness down [*sic*] the mountainside into the valley, bringing the creatures of the night (owls, bats, fireflies, but also porcupines) in its wake. These traverses are disguised, one assumes, to make the itemization of features of the landscape a less contrived-seeming procedure. The centre of the poem, however, consists of an undisguised prospect sequence. The poet ascends the hillside to his "wonted seat." From there,

> Spread out below in sun and shade,
> The shaggy Glen lies full displayed . . .
> And through it like a dragon spread,
> I trace the river's tortuous bed.

The eye then follows the river, noting flora and fauna on the way, into the setting sun.

In adhering to the conventions of the picturesque in topographic poems like "Evening Rambles," Pringle seems to be entirely untroubled by the question Burchell raises: whether the great aesthetic schemas of European landscape art have universal applicability. Pringle's own use of the word *picturesque* is loose:

> The general aspect of the country [around Albany in the Eastern Cape] was . . . fresh, pleasing, and picturesque. The verdant pastures and smooth grassy knolls formed an agreeable contrast with the dark masses of forest which clothed the broken ground near the river courses. The undulating surface of the champaign country was moreover often agreeably diversified with scattered clumps or thickets of evergreens interspersed with groves of large trees, like a nobleman's park. . . . In the lower bottoms, wherever a brook or fountain had been discovered, . . . we found the emigrant at work in his field or garden; his reed hut or wattled cabin generally placed on the side of some narrow ravine, under the shade of a grove or thicket. . . . These cabins often looked extremely handsome and picturesque, as we came suddenly in sight of them peeping out from the skirts of the ancient forest, or embowered in some romantic wood or evergreen shrubbery.[4]

Pringle uses the word as a cultivated layman rather than an artist would, to cover typical (even clichéd) elements of picturesque landscape, and indeed, in this passage, as a kind of shorthand for scenes that put the spectator in mind of England, where to a great extent landscape gardening had remade the country park in the image of picturesque art.

Pringle's residence in South Africa was limited to Cape Town and the Eastern Cape. He did not therefore face as directly as

---

4. *Narrative of a Residence in South Africa* 105–06. For other "picturesque" moments in the *Narrative*, see 7, 31, 84.

Burchell the problem of representation raised by the interior plateau, and particularly by the flat, arid Karoo—the problem, to put it in its crudest form, of finding enough in the landscape to fill the painting or the poem; or, to put it in a different way, of finding an art form responsive to "empty" country. The word that Pringle uses in what appears to be a complementary sense to "picturesque" is "wild";[5] there is also a passage in which he contrasts the "sublimely stern" scenery of the Eastern Cape coast with the "tameness" of English scenery (7). In his extremely loose usage, we therefore have the *wild/sublime* set against the *tame/picturesque;* in "Evening Rambles" this opposition is actualized as one between mountain and valley.

What is striking in both Burchell and Pringle is how little the possibility is explored of deploying the rhetoric of the sublime upon the interior plateau. Why, at a time when the notion of the sublime had not exhausted its potency, was it not applied to the vast "empty" spaces of the hinterland?

The Wilderness and the Sublime

"The wilds," "the wilderness" are resonant words in the Judaeo-Christian tradition. In one sense, the wilderness is a world where the law of nature reigns, a world over which the first act of culture, Adam's act of naming, has not been performed. The origins of this conception of the wilderness lie in pre-Israelite demonology, where the wilderness (including the ocean) was a realm over which God's sway did not extend. But a second sense of the wilderness grew up in Judaeo-Christian theology: the wilderness as a place of safe retreat into contemplation and purification, a place where the true ground of one's being could be rediscovered, even as a place as yet incorrupt in a fallen world (G. Williams 5). Both of these potentially conflicting conceptions of the wilderness have played a part in the history of South Africa. The first can be loosely associated with British colonialism and the effort to maintain a border separating a region of

---

5. See, for example, *Narrative* 7, 84, as well as "Evening Rambles," "The Desolate Valley."

order and culture—the Colony—from the barbarian wilderness. The second can, just as loosely, be associated with Afrikaner isolationism; though we should note how strictly the Calvinist theology of the Afrikaner, while blessing the analogy of colonial hinterland with biblical Promised Land, blocks the further analogy of hinterland with Eden. Thus in W. E. G. Louw's long poem about the Creation, Adam is brought to life in a garden filled not with African flora but with roses, saffron, rosemary. The great garden poem in Afrikaans, Ina Rousseau's "Eden," speaks of Eden as longed-for but failed, lost, remote:

> Staan daar nog 'n Eden êrens,
> verwaarloos soos 'n stad in puin,
> gedoem tot langsame verrotting
> deur eeue die mislukte tuin?

> [Does an Eden still stand somewhere,
> abandoned like a city in rubble,
> doomed to gradual decay,
> ages long the failed garden?]

Thomas Pringle, gazing at the Knysna coast from the deck of the ship bringing him to Africa, saw "lonesomeness and dreary wildness" (*Narrative* 7). In later South African topographic writing we continue to find the interior of the country assimilated into the figure of the waste land, a land of

> scorching sun, . . . withering wind, . . . serpent's tooth . . .
> vulture swoop, . . . locust cloud . . .
> [and] faithless mocking phantom [i.e., mirage]
>   [Dugmore, "A South African Wilderness"]

> Wilderness, sterile and parched, far-stretching away to the
>   skyline,
> Desolate, stone-freckled waste, gaunt and inclement Karroo,

writes Francis Carey Slater ("The Karroo"). In F. D. Sinclair's "Christmas Night 1944," travellers into the interior are "lost beneath the cruel / And blazing jewellery of the Cross"—lost, that is, beneath the constellation presiding over the southern wilderness, the indifferent and perhaps even demonic inverse of the cross of salvation. This conception of the wilderness as a realm

sundered from God is not wholly absent from Afrikaans topographic poetry:

> Eindloos wyd strek doods en kaal
> Verskroeide vlaktes waar die stofson straal

> [Endlessly wide, deathly and bare, stretch
> Scorched flatlands where the dust-sun glares],

writes S. Ignatius Mocke in a poem ("Die Vrystaat" [The Free
State]) that offers no redeeming contrast to barrenness—no water, no salvation. When the hot *bergwind* blows, the comfortable
dwellers along the coastal strip, in Peter Blum's poem, smell

> droogte en brand, en gerug
> van sprinkaan, aardbewing en oproer
> op daardie skroeiende binnelandse lug
> —dan, dan
> weet ons op watter vasteland ons boer.
>> ["Nuus uit die binneland"]

> [drought and fire, and rumour
> of locust, earthquake and unrest
> on that scorching inland air
> —then, then
> we know on what continent we are settled.]
>> [News from the Interior]

The topos of the interior as a wilderness is thus common
enough in South African literature. The development we might
have expected, however, had the European model been followed—namely, the reclamation of this nameless wilderness, or
what aspects of it are amenable to reclamation, in the name of
the sublime—never occurred. In Europe those features of the
landscape that were once regarded as a wilderness, forever useless to man and therefore (in what may seem a paradox to us)
unnatural—the Alps, for instance—were by 1800 viewed as sublime par excellence. It was Shaftesbury who in 1709 first proposed that the effects on the spectator of soaring heights, plung-
ing abysses, and savage prospects belonged under the ancient
category of the sublime; Burke, in the 1750s, in effect estab-

lished the sublime as a major aesthetic category side by side with the beautiful (Noyes 35, Thacker 77–78). The beautiful, the sublime, and, for a while, the picturesque were three great categories under which specimens of European landscape were classified; these categories, or at least the first two, remained so fundamental to European aesthetic experience that they even organized the way in which landscape was seen. I have already noted evidences in Burchell and Pringle of the picturesque as a mode of organizing the representation, pictorial and literary, of the South African landscape. But why was the sublime, a grander and at first sight more inclusive category, resorted to so little?

To begin with, in European art the sublime is far more often associated with the vertical than the horizontal, with mountains than with plains. The fenlands of East Anglia were shunned by eighteenth-century tourists, who flocked instead to the Scottish Highlands or the Lake District (Watson 22). No doubt part of the attraction of the vertical to the painter is that the vertical is the plane of the painting itself as it is hung; but sublime art goes on to make verticality—heights and depths—the locus of important—"profoundly" important—feelings such as fear and ecstasy, and values such as transcendence and unattainability (Weiskel 24)—values occasionally attached to skies but never to land expanses. Wordsworth called sublimity "the result of Nature's first great dealings with the superficies of the earth" (*Guide* 181), not considering that plains, as well as mountains and oceans, resulted from these dealings. In book 7 of *The Prelude* (1805) he writes of mountainous regions as the regions where "simplicity and power [appear] most obviously," where by "influence habitual" they may "[shape . . . the soul/To majesty" (720–26). In 1850 he adds the desert as another soul-shaping environment, but limits it to shaping the soul of the Arab (7.747–49). As he remarks in the *Guide,* even sublime impressions "cannot be received from an object however eminently qualified to impart them, without a preparatory intercourse with that object or with others of the same kind" (359)—that is to say, whatever its sublime possibilities, the South African plateau cannot be expected to strike travellers fresh from England as sublime. (I do not imply, of course, that travellers did not find the plateau at all striking though I find no evidence to substantiate John Povey's claim that "its impact [was of] shattering ferocity" [117].)

The language of the sublime is easily enough transposed to the mountains of South Africa, for example, by W. C. Scully in "Compass Berg." And the sublime possibilities of the veld do not go unremarked. Here is William Hamilton, c. 1917:

> The height, and the breadth and depth, and the nakedness
>   there! . . .
> The limitless outlook, the space, and the freedom beneath
>   [heaven].
>
> ["The Song of an Exile"]

Numerous other celebrations of the sublime limitlessness of the veld are to be found in such collections as E. H. Crouch's *Treasury of South African Poetry and Verse* (1909) and Francis Carey Slater's *Centenary Book of South African Verse* (1925). Roy Campbell, to whom the veld seemed not a positive limitlessness but "a gap in nature, time, and space" to be apprehended only in terms of its "vacuity" ("An Anatomy of the Veld"), satirizes the poetry of the sublime in his "Veld Eclogue":

> There is something grander, yes,
> About the veld, than I can well express,
> Something more vast—perhaps I don't mean that—
> Something more round, and square, and steep, and flat . . .
> Something more "nameless"—That's the very word!

In Afrikaans poetry there are similar instances of what I may call the first moment of the sublime, a moment at which an attempt to encompass the landscape in the imagination breaks down:[6]

> o hemelse gloed, tydlose glans bo hierdie wye
> grootse wêreld vol stilte en lig, lig sonder grens of soom
>
> [Uys Krige, "Verre blik"]

> [o heavenly lustre, timeless glow over this wide
> great world full of stillness and light, light without bound or
>   seam]
>
> [Far Gaze]

---

6. What I call the second moment of the sublime is, in Thomas Weiskel's scheme, the third stage (Weiskel 21–24).

O verre wydtes van die groot-oop dag . . .
[C. M. van den Heever, "O verre wydtes"]

[O far expanses of the great open day . . .]

But the cult of expansion, whether as an aesthetic-spiritual programme of the kind described by Marcus (52) and de Man (75–
77) or as a geopolitical ethos, was to be eclipsed by 1945. Poems
like the above, from the 1930s, came too late in the day to quicken
Afrikaans poetic art with new recognition of the sublime possibilities of the South African landscape. Similarly, though they bring
in Cubism and Futurism in highly original ways to suggest lines of
force and tension in nature, J. H. Pierneef's scenes of empty
plains, blank mountains, and towering skies, painted in the 1920s,
have had few imitators outside the realm of *Kitsch,* probably because of their tendency to heroicize the landscape.

I have mentioned the first moment of the sublime. What
might a possible second moment be? The account given by Kant
in section 27 of the *Critique of Aesthetic Judgment* runs as follows.
The imagination, confronted with a sublime natural spectacle,
finds itself unable to represent it: the spectacle exceeds all measure (all comparison), is in this sense absolute. The failure of the
imagination creates a mixture of astonishment and anxiety in the
subject, making up half of what Burke calls the "delightful horror, which is the most genuine effect, and truest test of the
sublime" (88). But what is the source of the other half, delight?
Kant's answer is that it lies in our recognition, concurrent with
our reaction of fear, that there exists within us a standard which
the imagination, as a faculty based on the senses, has failed to
measure up to, namely, the idea of the transcendent. The very
incapacity of the sensuous imagination, occurring together with
the realization that the mind has a standard by which it is capable
of measuring that incapacity, is then reconceived as an evidence
and a symbol of the relation of the mind to a transcendent order.
That is, the sublime originates when conventional readings of
landscape break down, but in their collapse recognizes the founding of another order of meaning (Kant 106–07; Weiskel 22).

What is subsequently made of this second moment of the sublime can be, as Thomas Weiskel points out, extremely various.

"An ideological component necessarily enters. . . . What happens to you standing at the edge of infinite spaces can be made, theoretically, to 'mean' just about anything" (28). For some observers, a plenitude of meaning seems to stream from confrontation with the inordinately vast. In the poem by Krige I have quoted from, attributes of strength and freedom are read out of the sublime landscape and then transposed (or wished) upon the people who inhabit it. To C. M. van den Heever the vast, wide-open skies unveil a transcendent destiny from which man is sundered by his mortal nature. For an observer like Campbell, on the other hand, the confrontation with vast, empty spaces yields only banality.

South African poetry reads a diversity of meanings out of the spaciousness of the landscape, but does not invoke the aesthetic of the sublime powerfully enough or early enough in history to create a standard to be either adhered to or reacted against. That is to say, a certain way of feeling about the landscape in which awe weighs heavily did not become the norm. As to why the sublime did not flourish in nineteenth-century South Africa, we can conclude only that this was a matter of historical circumstance. There was no tradition of landscape painting or writing—indeed no artistic tradition at all—among the Dutch at the Cape, among whom, anyhow, religious certainties seem to have been unquestioned enough to make substitute transcendencies like the sublime unnecessary (Weiskel correctly calls the sublime "a massive transposition of transcendence into a naturalistic key" [4]). And among Englishmen travelling in the interior, the amount of topographical writing of any talent or ambition was exceedingly slim.

The position one should be wary of taking up, however, is that the sublime *could* never have taken root in British South Africa, either because by the turn of the nineteenth century it was a concept in desuetude or because it could not have endured the transplantation. A contrasting look at the landscape arts in nineteenth-century America and at the interaction of European tradition with native topography there will not only indicate some of the potential of the sublime outside Europe, but suggest what South African landscape description did *not* become.

American Landscape

Of course nineteenth-century American landscape painting is not (as in South Africa) the work of visitors nurtured on European scenery and trained in a European landscape tradition, but of painters born in America, receiving their initial training there, for the most part visiting Europe only after developing a personal style. As such they have no parallel in nineteenth-century Africa. Nevertheless, they paint within a European aesthetic tradition, and the conflicts they face between a European aesthetic and an American subject are of the same kinds as—though on a considerably greater scale than—the conflicts adumbrated in Burchell.

Rather than attempting a survey of nineteenth-century American landscape art, I will confine myself to two topics of direct relevance to the case of South Africa: the picturesque and the sublime; and the treatment of water, atmosphere, and light.

One of the premises of the discussion thus far has been that landscape (as opposed to terrain) is always viewed through the medium of a schema of representation, of which the simplest example is the rectangular frame; or, to be more precise, that an interaction takes place between the spectator's schema and the scene before his eyes. The life cycle of schemas—of which the picturesque is one—is that, beginning by opening up new possibilities of representation, they typically end by closing off possibilities into a single vision. The beginnings of American landscape art are synonymous with the Hudson River School; and the history of the Hudson River School can be written as, first, an effort to visualize American reality within the schema of the picturesque, and thereafter—largely in the name of the sublime—to liberate it from the conventions of the picturesque. The interaction between the Claudian picturesque and the efforts of early American art to free the American landscape into greater imaginative potency can usefully be narrowed down to the treatment of distance. The serene and luminous remote distances of Claude can be felt—and were certainly so felt by Claude's contemporaries—to preserve a space for the numinous in a world rapidly becoming desacralized (Wolf 197–98). Indeed, it was the particular achievement of the picturesque to find a way of uniting a neoclassical nostalgia for an ideal past landscape with a Romantic yearning for sources of transcendence in the natural world. The picturesque was thus a singularly effective, if temporary, solution to a spiritual and imaginative crisis undergone by Europe in the late eighteenth century. What made the picturesque congenial to America was that, as adapted, it provided means for expansive drives to play themselves out in the theatre of the American outdoors. From the late 1840s, when Thomas Cole showed how a break with whatever was formulaic in the picturesque could be achieved (Novak 77–78), until the 1880s, American landscape art was centred not only on the treatment of distance but on distance itself. The following comment by Howard Mumford Jones, though overly rhetorical, is true to its spirit:

> Beyond the farm, or the village, or the church, or the meadow, or the fishing pool, or the picnic spot, or the park, there lies a vast, extended nature—shimmering skies, a mysterious mist, mountains that block the view, vistas that compel the eye to climb upward through the picture and lose itself in a vague and immense distance. [362]

The so-called luminism of the later Hudson River School (Fitz Hugh Lane, John Kensett, Martin Johnson Heade), in whose work a pale light seems to emanate from the distance and envelop the entire landscape in clarity, can be seen as a lyrical extension of this concern with an ideal centre that is simultaneously far away and everywhere present. Though all the technical preconditions seemed to exist in the 1850s for a native American Impressionism, its growth was forestalled, Barbara Novak suggests, by the pursuit of the far-off manifested in luminism (91). In this sense, luminism represents a late move from the picturesque toward the sublime, an assertion of the sublime possibilities of American landscape.

It would be misleading to say that the story of landscape art in the nineteenth-century United States is a story of the quest for the sublime. Nevertheless, the sublime, the American sublime, is the keynote of that art, however various in mood and temper the art is. Thus at the more confident end of the scale we might place the paintings of Frederic Church, landscapes so prehistoric as to be mythical, visions of an Edenic New World to which Church's public reacted with an enthusiasm that proved how well he gauged its hunger (Huntingdon 82), and the heroic Far Western gorges and peaks of Albert Bierstadt and Thomas Moran; at the other end we might place paintings like Heade's *Sunset on Long Beach,* with its overwhelmingly vast and empty sky, the first American instance of an "agoraphobic" response to boundlessness (Hawes 13).

The sublimity that American art discovers in (or projects into) the landscape is of course a reflection (or projection) of an ethos of progress and expansion. The landscape is vast, open, challenging; the element of anxiety we detect in Heade may reflect uneasiness about the ethos as much as oppression induced by vast spaces. The landscape is also dramatic. Over vast areas it is wooded, dark, mysterious. It is impossible to say whether American landscape emerges so dramatically on canvas because the topography "is" dramatic, or whether features of landscape are emphasized that invite dramatic treatment, just as it is futile to ask whether the South African landscape is so often represented as monotonous because it "is" monotonous, or because a preconception reigns that Africa is static, sunk in aeons of slumber, or indeed, as Burchell suggests, because an eye trained in Europe sees no variety in the veld. But there can be no doubt that atmospheric conditions in North America make possible, indeed invite not only dramatic skies but light full of change, variety, and contrast.[7] American landscape art increasingly takes note of weather. We know that Church played with dramatic oppositions of cool and warm atmosphere (Huntingdon 19). Cole's notations of the effects of weather on light become more and more precise. In his "Letters on Landscape Painting" (1855–56) Asher Durand writes of the complexity of "atmospheric space . . . under the influence of variable sky, cloud shadows and drifting vapor," of "all the subtleties of light with color subject to

7. This generalization does not hold for the arid Southwest United States—and American landscape art before the twentieth century signally fails in its rendering of the Southwest.

the media through which it passes, the intricacy of reflections from accidental causes" (Novak 89). Certainly in the phase of luminism the sky settles, or recedes, into a timeless glow; but luminism is impossible to conceive without the Hudson Valley topography of lakes and rivers, sheets of still water that reflect and amplify the luminosity of the skies. It is the component of water in the American landscape (surface water, atmospheric moisture), above any other feature, that makes possible a landscape of tension and transcendence.

I have assumed throughout that literary landscape, particularly nineteenth-century literary landscape, is a rendering of landscape visualized and composed in the mind's eye, and therefore that pictorial art gives the lead to topographic description. Broadly, American landscape writing of the period bears out this assumption.

The narratives of real-life travellers and explorers of the West—the journals of Lewis and Clark, for instance—contain detailed notes on the terrain but only rare and perfunctory attempts to see the landscape as a totality (for example, Lewis and Clark 132). In literary description, on the other hand, the emphasis falls more and more on versions of the sublime, which is usually associated with feelings of expansion and all-embracingness. The movement is surprisingly rapid. In 1835, Washington Irving is still trying to assimilate the prairies into the Claudian picturesque.[8] At virtually the same time the young Emerson is writing, "Standing on the bare ground,—my head bathed in the blithe air and uplifted into infinite space,—all mean egotism vanishes. I become a transparent eyeball; I am nothing; I see all; the currents of the Universal Being circulate through me; I am part or parcel of God" (11), and Whitman will soon by chanting "the chant of dilation" (49). In the heady years of Transcendentalism it is hard to find a landscape that is kept at a viewing distance from the eye, not ingested by it. In William Cullen Bryant's "The Prairie" we find this tension thematized: a tension

8. "The sunny [prairie] landscape [had] the golden hue of one of the landscapes of Claude Lorraine" (462).

betweeen a landscape out there, to whose autonomy some duty of representation is owed, and a landscape absorbed and fixed by the expansive eye:

> These are the gardens of the Desert, these
> The unshorn fields, boundless and beautiful . . .
> I behold them for the first,
> And my heart swells, while the dilated sight
> Takes in the encircling vastness. Lo! they stretch
> In airy undulations, far away,
> As if the ocean, in his gentlest swell,
> Stood still, with all his rounded billows fixed,
> And motionless forever.—Motionless?—
> No—they are all unchained again. The clouds
> Sweep over with their shadows, and, beneath,
> The surface rolls and fluctuates to the eye.

[118]

The spaciousness, grandeur, and sublimity of American landscape art, and the linking of physical expanses with expansiveness of soul, feeds and is fed by the popular conviction that American space is the natural environment of a race fitted for a spacious destiny. In the immensely successful album *The Home Book of the Picturesque,* published by Putnam in 1852, with essays by Irving, Cooper, and Bryant and engravings by Durand, Kensett, Church, and Cole, among others, is a long introductory essay entitled "Scenery and Mind" by E. L. Magoon. "Grand natural scenery tends permanently to affect the character of those cradled in its bosom," Magoon writes: "beauty and sublimity are thus . . . interfused and commingled with the whole substance of the mind." Thus people who grow up in hilly, rugged surroundings are independent, strong, and high-minded, while people of the "monotonous plains" are crouching, squalid, and brutal: "mere space, contemplated under the dome of heaven, prostrates, rather than sustains, the mind." Second only to mountains in its formative effect on character is the ocean; lakes too have their ennobling influence. The American scene, with its mountains, lakes, and forests and its long coastline, has formed the national character and "[confirmed] our destiny as a nation" (Deakin 25–26, 36, 3).

The link between landscape and national character is a prominent theme of nineteenth-century German nationalism, finding its most extreme expression in the writings of Wilhelm Heinrich Riehl, with their emphasis on the rootedness of a *Volk* in its native landscape (Mosse chap. 1). This *Volksideologie* certainly does not go without echo in South Africa. In the early, patriotic phase of Afrikaans poetry, in the first decades of this century, the task was explicitly laid upon the writer to find evidences of a "natural" bond between *volk* and *land,* that is to say, to naturalize the *volk*'s possession of the land. In the logic of similitudes elaborated in patriotic poetry, from the spaciousness of the land follows spaciousness of character; a landscape that invites freedom of movement promises freedom of personal and national destiny; wide horizons are a sign of an expansive future; and so forth. In these respects, first the United States and then South Africa rehearse familiar themes from the ideological repertoire of Western colonialism.

Landscape and History

There are two broad reasons why a sublime landscape art emerges so vigorously in the United States and in so late, tentative, and stunted a way in South Africa. First, topography, vegetation, and atmospheric conditions make the transposition of the sublime from Europe to whole regions of North America a more obvious step than from Europe to the South African interior. Second, the full ideological apparatus that accompanies expansive nationalism, including national arts, was in place by midcentury in the United States; while even allowing for the difference of scale, such an apparatus cannot be said to exist in South Africa before the 1930s, and then only as an adjunct of Afrikaner nationalism.[9] And, while it by no means follows that the sublime must be sympathetic to the politics of expansion, conquest, and grandeur,

9. John Povey provides a reading, perhaps more sympathetically disposed than mine, of early South African landscape poetry in English as a record of psychological adaptation by settler poets to a new natural environment and as an index of "changing sympathies and allegiances" that lead eventually to "sentiments of incipient nationality" (116).

it is certainly true that the politics of expansion has uses for the rhetoric of the sublime.

Neither the assertion nor (consequently) the questioning and denial of the sublimity of the South African environment therefore becomes an important issue in South African landscape art. Filling the vacuum is, instead, a concern with the hermeneutics of landscape. The dominating questions, particularly in poetry, and most of all in English-language poetry, become: How are we to read the African landscape? Is it readable at all? Is it readable only through African eyes, writeable only in an African language? Is the very enterprise of reading the African landscape doomed, in that it prescribes the quintessentially European posture of reader vis-à-vis environment? Behind these questions, in turn, lies a historical insecurity regarding the place of the artist of European heritage in the African landscape such as we do not encounter in America—an insecurity not without cause.

3

Farm Novel and Plaasroman

For two decades of this century, 1920–40, the Afrikaans novel concerned itself almost exclusively with the farm and *platteland* (rural) society, with the Afrikaner's painful transition from farmer to townsman. Of major English-language novelists, on the other hand, only Olive Schreiner (in *The Story of an African Farm*, 1883) and Pauline Smith (in *The Beadle*, 1926, and in the stories collected in *The Little Karoo*, 1925, rev. 1930) have taken farming life as their subject. By themselves Schreiner and Smith cannot be said to have defined a "farm novel" genre in English to parallel the *plaasroman* in Afrikaans. One might even argue that neither is a true farm novelist. As women, as people of English culture, as free thinkers, they perhaps stood too far outside the insular patriarchal culture of the Boer farm to write of it with true intimacy. The farm in Schreiner is perhaps too little distinguishable from nature, the farm in Smith too little distinguishable from the village. On the other hand, they approach the reality and the institution of the farm out of a literary tradition of their own, a tradition of the English novel of rural life. In their different ways, they conceive—indeed, cannot help conceiving—the farm in a wider context than the Afrikaans farm novelist. At the very least they provide a foil to the *plaasroman*, throwing its preconceptions into relief.

Schreiner's African Farm

What kind of place is the African farm of which Schreiner's novel is the story? Schreiner's farm lies on a "wide, lonely plain," a "weary flat of loose red sand" (35, 38). The heavens above are as empty and indifferent as the earth. When the young Waldo offers up a burnt sacrifice to God, it is ignored. The terms describing it pile up: indifferent, empty, desolate, barren, wide, vast, monotonous; and if none of these, then perhaps "something more 'nameless'—That's the very word!" We are in the midst, as Roy Campbell's gibe reminds us, of one of the topoi of South African literature: the veld as the site of wholesale absence, in this case the absence above all of a personal God.

Besides having a topography—limitless plain beneath limitless sky (though because it has no structure, no detail, no variety, no articulation, this topography cannot be read)—Schreiner's Karoo has a chronography extending from prehistory to a posthistory after man. In this chronography, the life spans of individuals and even of peoples constitute negligible intervals.

There is a second scale of nonhuman time and distance on the farm too, by whose measure the plants and insects of the Karoo live. A pulsing and complex life goes on in the monotonous red sand, generations passing away, empires rising and falling within the space of a season.

Somewhere intermediate between the infinitesimal and the infinite, the farm tries to assert its own measure of time and space by which to carry on its self-absorbed existence. This existence the covalent cosmic and microcosmic scales show up as absurd, of no more intrinsic importance than the goings-on of snakes and spiders.

Thus far we have seen nothing to distinguish Schreiner's farm from raw nature: it is undomesticated, and, at the level I have been describing, indomesticable. But the farm is also a place of human habitation, and indeed so human in its bigotry, hypocrisy, and idleness that all that redeems it from being an African town in miniature is its setting in nature. The farm thus has two aspects: nature and town. These aspects merely coexist. They form no synthesis.

Because the African farm has a split nature, it is impossible to live an integrated life upon it. Either one lives on the inhospitable land (as Waldo tries to do) and perishes or one lives in the farmhouse and succumbs at last to adulthood, becoming another Tant' Sannie, counting one's money, counting one's sheep. For the farmhouse is at war with nature. The children who bring the germ of nature into the house (Waldo, Lyndall) have it thrashed out of them. As for the blacks, the Bushmen who lived in nature (in caves, not in huts) have been exterminated, while those Hottentot and Kaffir women absorbed as servants by the farmhouse have grown as stupid and heartless as their mistress.

This African farm is, then, Schreiner's microcosm of colonial South Africa: a tiny community set down in the midst of the vastness of nature, living a closed-minded and self-satisfied existence, driving out those of its number who seek the great white bird Truth by venturing out into the unexplored veld or by reading outside the One (closed) Book. The farm is pettiness in the midst of vastness.

Since it is clear that Schreiner does not take on the task of comprehensively representing a South African sheepfarm, it would be unfair to demand this of her. Nevertheless, the story that emerges from her pen is slanted, one-sided. There is an alternative story of the farm we can conceive, a story Schreiner does not tell, a story to be identified with Old World farming rather than with farming in the colonies. In such a story, the farm is not simply a house or settlement in a fenced space, but a complex: at one and the same time a dwelling place, an economy, and all the creatures that participate in that economy, in particular the members of the family (in however extended a sense) who both own the farm in law and are owned by the farm—owned in that they owe it their truest labour, their livelihood, and ultimately their lives.

In this story, the farmer has both rights and obligations. However absolute his ownership, he has duties to the land, to his heirs (as well as, to a lesser extent, to his forebears), and even to the ecology of the farm—that is, to the farm as part of nature. He is, in the language of myth, forbidden to rape the land.

Instead he must husband it, giving it a devoted attention that will bring it to bear manyfold, yet keep it fertile for succeeding generations. In the logic of the myth, the sons who inherit the farm husband the same land; or, to put it in another way, the generations of husband-farmers are the same (mythic) man.

Where does Schreiner stand in relation to this venerable Old World conception of farming? The answer is that she follows the myth only negatively. Her farm is reigned over not by a man but by a sterile and slothful woman; it yields (or is made to seem to yield) nothing (it is typical of Schreiner's writing, intensively realized in some places, sketchily in others, that Tant' Sannie should prosper while so little productive work is evident on the farm). Insofar as there is life in the veld, it is not the life of sheep—which stand about sluggish and heat-stunned—but the life of insects. In fact, from the sight the reader is given of the economy of farming it is difficult to see how the possession either of land as barren as this or of sheep can constitute real (as distinct from symbolic) wealth.

Rather than taking Schreiner's farm as a realistic representation of an African stock farm, I suggest we should read it as a figure in the service of her critique of colonial culture. Whereas in the Old World model the farm is naturalized by being integrated with the land, and in turn historicizes the land by making the land a page on which the generations write their story, Schreiner's farm is an unnatural and arbitrary imposition on a doggedly ahistorical landscape. Schreiner is anticolonial both in her assertion of the alienness of European culture in Africa and in her attribution of unnaturalness to the life of her farm. To accept the farm as home is to accept a living death.

Harmonie

In the Aangenaam valley [Pleasant valley] . . . men and women still retained the old customs which had already died out elsewhere.—The Beadle 81

While Schreiner's Great Karoo farm is ahistorical, Smith's Little Karoo is firmly historical—indeed, so historical that it follows traditions that have perished everywhere else. In fact, though the Aangenaam valley is initially presented as poor, waterless, and "desolate" (7–8), its desolation is soon forgotten and it becomes a kind of Eden, producing a modest abundance, presided over by a benign *seignor,* in which it is possible to live as Andrina Steenkamp does, in prelapsarian innocence. The mythic values that accumulate around the valley are those of the womb: closure ("shut in between the Teniquota mountains and the Aangenaam hills") and fruitfulness. When Andrina visits the Great Karoo, on the other hand, she finds "overpowering and desolating" its flatness, openness, sterility (256–57).[1]

The farm of Harmonie, at the heart of the valley, is presented as the culmination of a historical tradition. Indeed, there would be nothing in *The Beadle* to indicate that Harmonie is not the *end* of history—the achievement of an ideal equilibrium or stasis or finality in social relations such as could survive forever—were it not for a pervasive tone of nostalgia, hinting that the idyll of Harmonie belongs to the past.

What is the history that Smith claims for Harmonie? The first Van der Merwe, we learn, was a "landrost" [*sic*] (magistrate) in the service of the Dutch East India Company, who brought with him from the Netherlands household articles that have been passed down in the family. During the eighteenth century, family slaves "trained to copy the work of European or Batavian masters" make furniture, doors, window-frames, which go into the building and furnishing of Harmonie (18,100). To the extent that it is possible to be venerable in South Africa, Harmonie has the venerability of the old Dutch homesteads of the Cape.

Harmonie preserves the best of the domestic tradition of the Dutch *middenstand:* "scoured cleanliness . . . dazzling polish . . . deep, rich colouring" (19). As for its present owner, "Stephan Cornelius van der Merwe [was] . . . just, generous and patient . . . [with] a quiet nobility of carriage. . . . [He] seldom spoke yet spoke always with authority" (39). Under his benign authority and/or

1. The Great Karoo is most desolate of all in the story "Desolation," in *The Little Karoo.* From topographical hints in the text, the setting of the story seems to be the Koup, the most arid stretch of the Karoo. When Smith writes of the Great Karoo she appears to have the Koup in mind.

patronage exists a varied community: tenant farmers like Aalst Vlokman, recipients of his charity (Johanna and Jacoba Steenkamp), the part domestic help, part adopted child Andrina, who lives "as one of the family" (24), guests like the Englishman Henry Nind. The Van der Merwes have built on their farm a church for the people of the valley. The mill and the post office are on their property; if the Jew woman's store is not (the text is not specific on this point), it is at least adjacent to it.

Harmonie is thus both a farm and the hub of the Aangenaam community. The valley has to come to it for the Sacrament, for shop goods, for communications. If there is no jail on the farm, that is because this Eden has, as yet, no call for one.

Not only does Harmonie provide the substructure of community in the valley, but, when we see communal feeling manifested, it is manifested at Harmonie: joy at the arrival of the post-cart, a "deep low hum of life" during the thanksgiving ceremony (82). At supper-time the farmhouse brings together the Van der Merwe family and their guests with their servants in more intimate domestic community.

Of course the construction of Harmonie as the Eden in the isolated valley is only a prelude to the entry of the serpent, Henry Nind, from whom Andrina-Eve's skulking, undeclared father cannot protect her because he cannot face the consequences of confessing his sin (expulsion from an Eden than which "no spot on earth [was] more dear" to him [274]). Nevertheless, even if sin is always already-there in the valley, in the form of Vlokman's guilty secret, it is only Vlokman himself who is excluded, by the state of his soul, from full participation in a way of life realized all around him in social and economic relations. In other words, it may be impossible for the guilty heart to live in Harmonie/Eden, but Harmonie nevertheless exists, and indeed, even after the unveiling of Nind, the confession of Vlokman, the shame of Andrina, the death of Jacoba, goes on existing. Eden survives; Andrina can be welcomed back into it, with her redeemed father and her blameless child.

So central is the place of Harmonie in *The Beadle* that we need have no qualms about taking it as Smith's African farm, and asking what kind of place she has invented.

The first thing to say is that Smith does not call it an African or even a South African farm. In fact the word *Africa* is not used in the book. Harmonie is not in South Africa but in the Little Karoo; not in the Little Karoo but in the Aangenaam valley. Smith's book is, at most, about the Little Karoo, as the stark contrast of her Great Karoo should warn us. Harmonie is a *regional answer* (from which it does not necessarily follow that *The Beadle* is a regional novel).

But if Harmonie is an answer, what is the question to which it responds? It is a question about the ideal rural order. What should the rural order be? Should it be an order of atomic farms, each with a patriarch ruling over (1) a wife, (2) sons, (3) daughters, (4) tenants, (5) servants, (6) beasts, and (7) the land, all relations having their translations into terms of money and being capable of being mediated through the law? Smith had sketched such an order in two stories in *The Little Karoo*. In "The Sisters" a farmer treats his daughters as assets to be exchanged for land (in fact not even for land but for the mortgage deed on the land which was the price he had paid for a lost case at law—the chain of exchanges stretches far back). In "The Father" a farmer uses his wife's body as a means to get himself unpaid labour: on her he will multiply himself, and each son she bears will in turn multiply the yield of his land. The story "Desolation" reflects the same order: an old woman is left to die because she is no longer productive.

The order sketched in these stories is thus one in which men inherit power when they take over the farm and proceed to rule in an absolute way over family, tenants, and land (over servants too, we presume, though servants in Smith tend not to be visible), their power being mediated through money. It is an order we can call patriarchal capitalism, though the capitalism is at an embryonic stage.

Though the conception of wives and children as capital is not foreign to the world of *The Beadle*, it is there treated with a certain lightness. More important, relations are not mediated through money because money is little used in the valley, which still enjoys a barter economy. And although Stephan van der Merwe inherits authority, he shares sway with his wife, waiving many of the powers of patriarchy. Each of his children, at the appropriate age, receives his or her independence. "Though family life among her people might still be, to a large extent, patriarchal, to each of her sons and daughters in turn Alida van der Merwe had granted such freedom as this" (240).

Authority, the power of the patriarchy, the power of capital, is thus withheld or deferred; it is present in the valley, but only as a shadow. (Yet who is to say that the son who succeeds to Harmonie will not be a despot?)

As for the substance of the social order, this is clearly pre-capitalist and based on duties. What origin Smith ascribes to the principle of dutifulness is not clear. It may be that God stands as the origin and that Harmonie is a model Christian community. Certainly Stephan van der Merwe's most obviously fulfilled duty is the building of a church for his people, and certainly evening prayer is the time for the bringing together of the extended Van der Merwe family. But the religion we see in *The Beadle* is confined to the devout performance of duties. One might well argue that the institution of duties itself is the ultimate principle—in other words, that the Aangenaam valley is an ideal community not necessarily because it follows God but because it follows its code of duties religiously.

The primary duty of the people toward their *seignor* is obedience: "Make me to be obedient to my mistress" and "Make me run quickly when my master calls" are the prayers of the two indentured servant children (204). On the side of the Van der Merwes the corresponding duty is charity. Out of charity outsiders like the "orphan" Andrina and the invalid Nind are taken into the wider family of clients, *bywoners* (tenant farmers), and servants.

The opposed models of the rural order that Smith presents in her two books are thus: (a) one in which ties of blood are discounted and all human relations, even those within the family, are mediated through money; and (b) one in which money is not the measure of all things, and human relations are conceived of as family bonds of greater or lesser degrees of closeness.

Peasant Farming and Peasant Culture

I have noted some features of *The Beadle* which suggest that the Aangenaam valley is precapitalist in organization. Let me recapitulate them and add a few more.

1. The life of the (extended) family and the economy of the farm are closely integrated.
2. Production is, by and large, for household use or for barter; money is little used.
3. Social mechanisms exist to counteract rather than encourage extremes of wealth and poverty.
4. Bonds of attachment exist between people and the soil.
5. Authority is patriarchal.
6. Marriage is looked upon as a universal life-goal. Marriages tend to take place early, and within the district. They are often arranged.
7. The community is culturally homogeneous.

The features I have listed are common to what, following Alan Macfarlane, I call classic peasant social organization (32–33). But the overlap is not complete. Certain features of classic peasant life are eschewed by Smith, while other aspects of life in the Aangenaam valley distinguish it from the classic pattern.

The feature added by Smith to which I would specifically point is hierarchy. There is a social scale extending from the Van der Merwes, with their traceable genealogy, down to Andrina, who does not know her parentage. On the other hand, in the classic mode, (1) the labour of the farm is wholly or largely performed by the family, hired help being rare; and (2) patriarchal authority goes hand in hand with a low status for women and a tendency for sons (and daughters-in-law) to live well into maturity under the parental roof. Both of these features are absent from Harmonie, and both departures are revealing.

The first, silence about the place of black labour, is common not only to Schreiner and Smith but, by and large, to the Afrikaans *plaasroman,* and represents a failure of imagination before the problem of how to integrate the dispossessed black man into the idyll (or in Schreiner's case the anti-idyll) of African pastoralism.

The second departure is peculiarly Smith's. I take the reign of the Van der Merwes to be her vision of a patriarchalism purged of its tyrannical side, a benign Little Karoo patriarchalism to be set against a malign Great Karoo patriarchalism. Smith's benign vision of Harmonie has many of the characteristics of wish-fulfilment. For the present, all I would point to is a fact of peasant life: that wives and children are liberated from toil only when their labour is no longer vital to the prosperity of the farm. Therefore Smith's two departures are connected: the benign reign of Stephan van der Merwe, liberator of his family, must rest on his ability to replace the labour of his family with the labour of servants.

Thus far I have said only the obvious: that Smith's Aangenaam valley is based on a selective vision of precapitalist social and domestic life; and that her selective silence about hired labour, the labour obligations of sons, and problems of inheritance suggests that she has not thought her way fully through the dynamics of peasant economy.

More intriguing is the question of why there must be a *seignor*, why Smith did not envision, in her ideal valley, a society of more or less equal independent farmers with their various *bywoners* and tenants. For in creating her *seignor*, however benign, and despite her assurance that on feast days "rich and poor mingled together without distinction of class" (82), Smith reintroduces the devil of class into her African Eden.

To understand this move one should consider the kind of culture the Dutch colonists had created on the South African *platteland*. In his description of the state of the Cape Colony at the turn of the nineteenth century, John Barrow distinguishes those farmers who live "in a decent manner" (mainly what he calls "planters," wine-farmers of French descent) from "the true Dutch peasant, or boor," who, unlike the typical English farmer, tends to live in idleness, neglecting to exploit the potential of his land. Barrow's distinction is thus between the prosperous planter/agriculturalist and the shiftless pastoralist, whom he calls indifferently "the Dutch peasant" and "the African peasant" (1:27–29).

Barrow's term *peasant* for the frontier farmer never gained currency at the Cape. Yet the truth is that many of the differences between the frontier farmer and the European peasant are more apparent than real. If the frontier farmer seems more like the free landowner without rents or duties than like the peasant, we might point to the class of free peasants in Europe, who gained their freedom from duties in much the same way as the Dutch in South Africa: by colonizing new land (Blum 29). Again, the extensive use of indigenous labour certainly distinguishes the Dutch colonist from the European. Yet, because this was not labour paid for in cash, it did not necessitate the same concessions to the money economy as it would have in Europe. Indeed, because slaves/servants, though not absorbed socially, were absorbed into the bottom of the family economy, one might go so far as to argue that the African farm represents an extension of the classic peasant household model rather than a divergence from it. Finally, if the typically extensive pastoral properties of the Dutch colonists seem very unlike the small, even minute agricultural holdings of European peasants, we might remind ourselves of the barrenness of these African tracts.

If there is reason, then, for thinking of the African farm as a transplanted peasant farm, adapted to Africa, we might also experiment with thinking of the culture of the African farm as a peasant culture. The features of the farm that Schreiner rejects—suspicion of the new, conformism, anti-intellectualism, narrow materialism—are typical features of peasant culture. In imagining Harmonie, might Smith not be shying away from a similar cultural ambience—an ambience which her earlier stories to some extent reflect?

The literature of the dying rural order, in South Africa as in Europe, is full of stories of sons and daughters who, once they have had a taste of urban life, look back on the peasant order into which they were born as unrelieved oppression. This is not strange. Peasant communities across the world are by their nature closed. Their values are homogeneous and conservative; their typical response to new ideas is to close themselves off to them. Because their mode of production requires a low level of mastery of a wide range of skills, they exhibit, in Marx's words, "no diversity of development, no variety of talent, no wealth of social relationships" (quoted in Shanin 230). Those people with a wider life-experience who move into peasant society—typically clergymen and schoolteachers—find themselves socially isolated.

Peasant culture is essentially static and employs a range of exclusions and sanctions to maintain itself in stasis. Judged from the outside, and particularly from the position of an educated person, however sympathetically disposed, peasant culture can justify its manifold internal oppressions, of beasts as of women and children, only as long as it maintains an ethos of work. The spectacle of peasant idleness, a vacuous leisure supported by petty despotism, provokes wholly understandable moral outrage. As was evident to Barrow, in a culture where there is either work or nothing, where there are no arts, only crafts, leisure and idleness amount to the same thing. Even so sympathetic an observer of farming life as George Sturt writing about rural England of the 1880s is troubled by the vacuity of leisure on the farms, as economic changes began to create "free time." Change, he writes,

> has found the villagers unequipped with any efficient mental habits appropriate to the altered conditions, and shown them to be at a loss for interesting ideas in other directions. They cannot see their way any longer. . . . Life has grown meaningless, stupid; an apathy reigns in the village—a dull waiting, with nothing in particular for which to wait. [*Change in the Village* 133][2]

Living outside print culture, the peasant responds to the outrage or distress of a Barrow or a Sturt only with silence.

All too often the townsman in fact approaches country life with a certain unstated demand that it be edifying, and is disappointed when it is not. Intellectuals (as distinct from folk-artists) do not *emerge* from the peasantry: they receive their formation elsewhere—they are sent away to school—and then, if they do so at all, go back to the peasantry. Therefore every return to the farm tends to be a version of pastoral, sharing in the anxiety of (high) pastoralism about the moral justification of such a return.

2. On Smith's own reading of Sturt and other writers on the social history of the English countryside, see Voss, "Die Pêrels van Pauline" 113–14.

"[Pastoral] retirement from the world may symbolize a desire for contemplation and a lack of aspiration that is virtuous; but it may also be an indication of forgetfulness of high purpose, a dropping out of the race. . . . In that light, it is capable of being a retirement into sloth," writes Peter Marinelli (59). Put in another way: relapse into sloth is a betrayal of the high pastoral impulse. For this reason the question of labour is central in all writing about country life. If there is a single crucial difference between Schreiner's African farm and Smith's Harmonie, it is that the first is a place of sloth (and therefore a betrayal of Schreiner's own pastoral yearnings), while the second is a place of industry.

Return to the Land

The nostalgia for country life in *The Beadle* is not, of course, unique to Smith. It is a feature of a great deal of writing in England in the years up to 1939. If we must put a *terminus a quo* to the back-to-the-country mood in England, we might follow W. J. Keith and date it to the "urban-rural dissociation of sensibility" of the 1880s (150). The causes of this break were economic and technological changes on an epochal scale. Before the break, the life of the traditional small-farming community was simply one way of life among many; after the break it came to be seen as a dying way of life and therefore, paradoxically, as a life-style to be conserved and imitated (see Jan Marsh, *Back to the Land*). The difference between before and after can be most clearly seen if we set side by side Richard Jefferies and George Sturt, born only fifteen years apart. Jefferies writes without a hint that the way of life he describes is doomed; whereas in Sturt, despite his sympathy for the old village culture (what he calls its "thrift"), the stance of the anthropologist recording a threatened culture is as unmistakable as the undertone of sorrow (see particularly *A Farmer's Life*).

In the United States, where land has been plentiful and where there was never a native peasantry, the dynamics of pastoralism have been different, turning on the question of whether the farmer should treat the land as nurturing mother or object or rape (Kolodny 71). Nevertheless, the theme of the return to the land as the recovery of the self's best energies—the "Antaeus myth"—is central to the work, both fictional and nonfictional, of Louis Bromfield (22).

But it was in Germany, particularly the Germany of the period between the World Wars, that the literature of the return to the land flourished most prolifically. The statistics provided by Peter Zimmermann show production of the *Bauernroman* peaking in the years 1929–38, when nearly two hundred of the genre were published (Zimmermann, figure 6). Several uniquely German factors determined the strength of the *Bauernroman:* the attraction of Spengler's *Kulturpessimismus* for middle-class intellectuals and an accompanying rejection of the culture of the metropolis ("*Grossstadtfeindschaft*"); the hardships of the 1920s; and the Nazi-encouraged *Blut und Boden* policy (see Bergmann, Schweizer). But we cannot isolate the return to the *Boden* as peculiar to German circumstances. The Great Depression provoked alarm about rural depopulation and agitation for a return to the land in many countries; and in the novels of the Afrikaans writer C. M. van den Heever, particularly *Groei* (1933), an ideal much like that of the *Bauernroman* is pursued: enlightened patriarchy, instinctualism, tilling the soil as a quasi-religious act in a *Lebensraum* free from capitalistic relations, subject only to natural laws (see chapter 4).

Smith's pastoralism is unlike that of Van den Heever or the German *Bauernroman.* The essential difference is that, while the latter writers envisage a return to a peasant social order as a utopian programme (and while Bromfield envisages the spread of enlightened small farmers in the Jeffersonian mould), Smith (as Voss has pointed out in "Die pêrels van Pauline") attaches herself to an English tradition of more or less nostalgic pastoral celebration, a tradition that hopes for the conservation of the old rural values but has no ambition to throw the engine of history into reverse.

Once we see Smith in the context of English country-writing, it becomes clearer why in her Aangenaam valley so prominent a place is accorded to a nascent colonial aristocracy. For if we are looking for a model of a social order from which the more repugnant features of classic peasant society (principally patriarchy and its consequences) have been purged, an order moreover against which charges of idle living are not commonly levelled, we can find one in the picture of the enlightened large land-owner with his obedient clientele of copyholders, tenants, and cotters that is elaborated in the English Tory literary tradition.

To say this is merely to say that Smith, wishfully and ahistorically, transplants a model of the rural order from England to Africa. But there is a second level of wishfulness in her vision too. For, as it is wishful to see a Cape Dutch aristocracy in parallel to the English aristocracy, so it may be wishful to see an English peasantry parallel to the Dutch peasantry of Africa. The truth of the matter is that the idealization of a past feudal order of reciprocal duties goes back in England to at least the time of Jonson ("To Penshurst") and is even as early as then a reaction to the growth of a capitalist agricultural order (R. Williams 35). It is open to doubt whether there existed in England from the sixteenth century onwards anything that can legitimately be called a peasantry in the classic mould, with an economy based on family proprietorship. Alan Macfarlane goes so far as to express the same doubt about the existence of an English peasantry as far back as the thirteenth century. Statutes of 1290 gave to every freeman the right to "sell at his own pleasure his land and tenements." Freehold tenure of this order is diametrically opposed to the form of familial land-ownership found in peasant society. In addition, it was in England alone that the custom of primogeniture—a custom restricted to parts of northwestern Europe—penetrated down to the level of smaller landowners, making England unique in this respect. Primogeniture, again, is at odds with joint ownership (Macfarlane 83–89, 187; Thirsk). Finally, agricultural capitalism was so efficient and powerful in England that the class of petty freehold landowners was always small and disadvantaged, and, till 1914, growing steadily smaller and weaker as land was taken over by larger landlords (R. Williams 188–89; Lipson 370–76).

Thus the writer looking to England for a model of a sturdy peasantry with its own land rights, joined by a web of reciprocal duties to a similarly rooted local aristocracy, is inevitably driven to search farther and farther back in history, into a more and more misty past. The power of capital in the English countryside turned out to be irresistible; the true motive behind nostalgia for a past of peasants and masters is more than likely to be a wishful rejection of capital and its history.

The Plaasroman

Schreiner's African farm shows the ugly face of a mode of farming in which the desultory labour of a class of serfs ruled over by idle masters wins a living—of a kind—from the indifferent earth. From Schreiner's account, there is no reason to suppose that the reign of the Boer-woman and her class over the African veld should ever end. From such a reign Lyndall flees; in the face of it, Waldo perishes.

But, as we know, trouble was brewing even in the 1880s for the white proprietors of South Africa, trouble that has not ended a century later, whose effect it has been to drive or draw most of them to the towns and cities, leaving their farms in the hands of large landowners. Some of the reasons for this trouble were the increase of capital looking for secure investment, the growth of a transport network which opened new markets and made farming more profitable, inefficient farming on parcels of land that shrank with every generation, and the lure of city pleasures to the children of the patriarchs.

This crisis on the *platteland* forms the historical background to Smith's works. It is behind the *Little Karoo* stories; and though *The Beadle* presents itself as being set outside history, or at least before the time of crisis, the creation of Harmonie is clearly a response to questions in the air in the 1920s.

How did Smith's Afrikaans contemporaries respond to these questions? The first thing to note about the *plaasroman* writers—and here I would single out D. F. Malherbe, Jochem van Bruggen, Johannes van Melle, Mikro, C. M. van den Heever, and Abraham Jonker—is that they see the crisis in the *platteland* more explicitly than Smith does as a conflict between peasant and capitalist modes of production. The figure of the monied townsman, usually a merchant, sometimes a lawyer or doctor, more often than not Jewish, looking for viable farming operations in which to invest, is common (see Malherbe, *Die meulenaar;* Jonker,

Die plaasverdeling; Van Bruggen, *Ampie* part III; Van den Heever, *Gister*). Complementing the figure of the townsman with too much money is the figure of the peasant farmer who has barely emerged into the money economy, and who in order to win the capital that will place his farm on a competitive footing in the new Darwinian economy has to mortgage his own land or ask kinfolk to mortgage land on his behalf (*Die meulenaar, Die plaasverdeling;* Van den Heever, *Groei*).

Conflict between old (peasant) and new (capitalist) notions of the value of land is thus widely represented. This does not mean, however, that we always find a clear-sighted recognition that an epoch in the rural economy is occurring. More often than not the capitalist is portrayed as a scheming villain (the Jew in *Die meulenaar* whose excuse is that "business is business" [52]; the Jewish shopkeeper in *Die plaasverdeling* who lures the hapless hero into his web of credit), while the new need for money is simply attributed to a desire for the vicious gratifications offered by the "English" city (see the analysis of the crisis offered by Kasper Booysen in *Ampie* 1:76–78). In this way xenophobia or moralism or both triumph over analysis of forces, and the *plaasroman* comes closest to the reactionary *Grossstadtfeindschaft,* anticapitalism, anti-Semitism, and *Blut und Boden* ideology of the *Bauernroman.*

The *plaasroman* writer who stands out as most neutral in the conflict, least predisposed to uphold peasant values without question, is Abraham Jonker, who provides a fairly relentless representation, clearly indebted to Naturalism, of the decline and defeat of those least fitted to survive in the struggle of the peasantry to adapt to the jungle of capitalism. *Die trekboer* shows a defeated farmer struggling and failing to comprehend the money economy, refusing to adapt by selling his labour, losing patriarchal authority over his family, and succumbing to alcohol in the town.

But in his receptivity to the ideology of Darwinism, Jonker (otherwise a run-of-the-mill writer) is an exception. By and large, the programme espoused by the *plaasroman* is one of a renewal of the peasant order based on the myth of the return to the earth: "Where the slumbering might of all national cultures lies: [in] man with his ties to the earth, with which he is mystically united by a dark love . . . here is the soil of generation," writes C. M. van den Heever (*Die Afrikaanse gedagte* 16). Not only will the peasant proprietor and his sons and daughters recover their true selves by a return to the earth: their serfs too will come to recognize that town life is an aberration, that true happiness is to be found on the farm where they were born (this is the theme of Mikro's Toiings trilogy). The order of the farm is idealized as one in which "each one gets his portion . . . according to established custom, every manservant, every maidservant, and the neighbours too" (Malherbe, *Die meulenaar* 68).

The novelist who comes to grips most thoughtfully and analytically with the crisis of the end of the old peasant order is Johannes van Melle, in *Dawid Booysen*. In this *roman à thèse* the hero Booysen rejects the option of paying his work force wages (in order that the old bonds of reciprocity between master and servant may wither) and farming for profit in the new market economy. He puts his opposition to the new economic order into practice by turning the estate he has inherited into a "klein kooperasie," a small cooperative (244), with *bywoners* enjoying a fifty-year tenancy on their parcels and proprietor and tenants cooperating to make themselves independent of the larger economy, even to the extent of baking their own bricks and forging their own spades. "We must first ask what our own needs are, the needs of our people and the Kaffirs on our farms, of our beasts, and not think about the market," he says (198). And he marries a girl who, though she has roots in the country, is not shaped in the old mould: she reads agricultural journals and takes an interest in his schemes.

Booysen's community is in fact not adequately described as a "ko-operasie": it is meant to be the first of a network of Christian communities across the *platteland*, each constituted by a paternalistic landlord with a cluster of tenants and a further stratum of black serfs, all operating to as large an extent as possible outside the greater economy, their purpose being to protect the growing class of landless white peasants, as well as landless black serfs, from the rigours and temptations of the new capitalist order.

The book that may finally have "laid the ghost of the traditional South African pastoral" is, according to A. E. Voss, Nadine Gordimer's *The Conservationist* (1974) ("A Generic Approach to the South African Novel" 116). The pastoral solution to the question of how the white man shall live in South Africa is that he should retreat into rural independence; and its ghost is laid when, in Gordimer's novel, the dark side of farm life, its buried half, the black corpse in the garden, is at last brought to light.

Without wishing to minimize the achievement of *The Conservationist,* which is in every way a worthy follower of *The Story of an African Farm* in the antipastoral tradition, I would ask whether it is in the nature of the ghost of the pastoral ever to be finally laid. True, the silences in the South African farm novel, particularly its silence about the place of the black man in the pastoral idyll, and the silence it creates when it puts into the mouth of the black countryman a white man's words (as Mikro does in his Toiings trilogy), speak more loudly now than they did fifty years ago. Our ears today are finely attuned to modes of silence. We have been brought up on the music of Webern: substantial silence structured by tracings of sound. Our craft is all in reading *the other:* gaps, inverses, undersides; the veiled; the dark, the buried, the feminine; alterities. To a pastoral novel like *The Beadle* we give an antipastoral reading like the present one, alert to the spaces in the text (Where is God? Where is Africa?). Only part of the truth, such a reading asserts, resides in what writing says of the hitherto unsaid; for the rest, its truth lies in what it dare not say for the sake of its own safety, or in what it does not know about itself: in its silences. It is a mode of reading which, subverting the dominant, is in peril, like all triumphant subversion, of becoming the dominant in turn. Is it a version of utopianism (or pastoralism) to look forward (or backward) to the day when the truth will be (or was) what is said, not what is not said, when we will hear (or heard) music as sound upon silence, not silence between sounds?

4

The Farm Novels of
C. M. van den Heever

I

Under the custom of inheritance that prevailed in South Africa into the twentieth century, every son of a farmer might expect to inherit a share of the paternal farm. Since families were large, it followed inevitably that, once the frontier was closed, the practice of dividing the land would result in inheritances too small to be viable farms. This situation became a reality, in some parts of the country earlier than in others, about the turn of the present century.[1] The social problem of the emergence of a class of landless farmers was made more acute in the 1930s by years of poor rainfall, low wool prices, and general economic depression. Not unnaturally, the Afrikaans novel of the 1930s gave extended coverage to the phenomena of strife over inheritance (brother against brother, father against son, widow against children), conflict between farmers and land speculators, the hardening of class boundaries between the landed and the landless, the migration of impoverished rural Afrikaners to the cities, competition

1. In respect of the northwest Cape, see Van der Merwe 271–84. In respect of the Transvaal, see Thomsen 58.

between black and white labour on the mines and diggings or on the railways, and the threat to traditional values posed by the city (with its liquor, gambling, prostitution, and foreign ways) and by the penetration of novel forms of gratification into the countryside. Faced with what was more and more clearly an epoch in the history of the Afrikaner, Afrikaans novelists responded in diverse ways: they celebrated the memory of the old rural values or proclaimed their durability or elaborated schemes for their preservation; they tracked the forces of change to their origins in history (capitalism), society (the Jews), or the cosmic order (God's will, the indifference of the universe); they denounced the rapacity of the new class of speculators; they satirized the pettiness, selfishness, and lack of family feeling of the *verengelste* (anglicized) urban Afrikaner.

The waning of a dispensation in which every white male could expect to be an independent landowner was not unnaturally experienced as a tragic turn in history by the generation that found itself deprived and dispossessed. In the literature of the period we see, not surprisingly, efforts to dignify the disaster by claiming for the old dispensation an antiquity losing itself in the mists of time. We also see efforts to buttress Afrikaner patriarchalism in order that a heightened significance should be attached to the acts of the founding fathers, to maintaining their legacy and perpetuating their values. Thus we find the ancestors hagiographized as men and women of heroic strength, fortitude, and faith, and instituted as the originators of lineages (Afr. *families*). The farms they carved out of the wilds, out of primal, inchoate matter, become the seats to which their lineages are mystically bound, so that the loss of a farm assumes the scale of the fall of an ancient house, the end of a dynasty.

For an example of the values and powers that can be attributed to a family farm, consider *Somer (Summer)* by C. M. van den Heever, the most considerable of the farm novelists. The Du Preez brothers, Tom and Frans, and their married sister have each inherited a quarter of the ancestral farm Driefontein. There was once another brother, but he was forced to sell out. The purchaser of this fourth portion, Faan, waits like a patient spider for debt, falling prices, and natural disasters to force the remaining Du Preez to sell. Gloomily the brothers contemplate the future. In the old days, they think, the forefathers ("die oumense") could have as much ground as they wanted, but now "the ground grows smaller and smaller. . . . It is as if the ground is shifting under us." What will happen to their own children they do not know. They can only sit fast and hope for the best; the alternative is to sell out and look for work on the mines (168, 127, 157).

A freak hailstorm destroys Frans's crop, and Frans faces having to yield his quarter of Driefontein to Faan. "Driefontein in *his* hands," thinks Tom agrily—"Driefontein that has been in the family since the Great Trek!" It must not come to pass. He offers his brother money to tide him over the bad times: "Great-grandfather, Grandfather, Father and all the others would be shamed if we let the ground go." The farm must remain in the family; together the brothers face the future, resolved to "losboer" it (literally, farm it loose) from its debt (178, 190–91).

A summary of the kind I have made, by depriving the characters of the moral colouring the author has given them (Tom is forthright and passionate, Faan devious), tends to expose the lack of persuasive power of this particular plot and other plots revolving around the struggles of farmers to retain inherited property. Frans may be unfortunate to be hit by a hailstorm and may feel unhappy to have to sell his ground to pay his debts, but it is not obvious that it is an offence against the notion of justice that Faan should buy it from him. To turn the legal transfer of land from one farmer to another into a tragedy, Van den Heever must somehow establish a bond of natural right between a farm and the man who inherits it from its founders such as cannot exist between a farm and its mere purchaser. He must also argue that a system of credit which allows farmers to run up debts guaranteed by their property is inherently unnatural, in that it tends to permit an equation between a farm and a sum of money. Only when he has succeeded in establishing the value of the farm in transcendent terms can the conflict over ownership become a conflict of some grandeur between natural right and historical forces, rather than a merely personal squabble over who should live in the farm-house and who should go down the mine.

In the myth of natural right elaborated by Van den Heever, the founding fathers pay for the farm in blood, sweat, and tears, not in money: they hack it out of primeval bush, they defend it against barbarians, they leave their bones behind in its soil. Inher-ited ownership of the farm therefore becomes a sacred trust: to alienate the farm means to forsake the bones of the ancestors. Furthermore, the creditor who compels the sale of the farm to pay a mere monetary debt places himself outside the laws of piety. To emphasize the impiousness of such an act of dispossession, the creditor is often presented as a man with no visible ascendants and therefore no tradition of piety of his own: a Jewish immigrant trader, a lawyer from out of town, an upstart *bywoner* (tenant farmer), a *novus homo*.

One might ask whether, if in terms of this myth it is in some sense sacrilegious to sell an ancestral farm, it is also sacrilegious to *buy* a farm in whose soil the ancestors of another man lie buried. The answer seems to be that it is possible to enter with-out offence into the ownership of land—not only legal owner-ship but legitimate ownership, ownership in natural right—provided that one establishes one's ownership by signing the land with one's imprint as one signs a legal document with one's mark—a process that may take a lifetime. I am not aware, how-ever, that the *plaasroman* ever confronts the question of whether it is possible to establish natural right over a farm acquired against his will (as, for example, in enforced settlement of a debt) from a dispossessed "natural" owner.

The natural right that the originator of the lineage establishes by shedding his sweat or blood on the land does not, in itself, ensure that, if his descendants are forced to alienate the farm, the loss of the farm will constitute an offence against natural justice, a tragic occurrence. Natural right must be reestablished in each generation by good stewardship of the ancestral estate. To be a good steward (*vooruitboer* [literally, farm forward]) is to make the earth bring forth manyfold and the flocks increase; it is to consolidate the substructure of the farm; it is to build upon the inheritance. To be a bad steward (*agteruitboer* [farm backward]) is to merely subsist upon what the ancestors built or to allow the farm to go to rack and ruin or to slide spinelessly into debt or all of these. Good stewardship is the fullest utilization of one's energies and talents, and the bounty of the farm, for ends that transcend material gain, though material gain (as might be expected in a Calvinist culture) will provide a reliable measure of diligent stewardship.

Besides farming the land in a spirit of piety toward *voorgeslagte* and *nageslagte* (past and future generations), besides being a good steward, the farmer must also love the farm, love this one patch of earth above all others, so that his proprietorship comes to embody a marriage not so much between himself and the farm as between his lineage (*familie*) and the farm. Such a marriage, which must be exclusive (monogamous) and more than merely proprietorial, will entail that in good years the farm will respond to his love by bringing forth bountifully, while in bad years he will have to stand by it, nursing it through its trials. The final test that the bond between them is supramaterial will be passed when a mystic communion of interpenetration takes place between them, when farmer becomes *vergroeid* (intergrown, fused) with farm: "Never before had he felt such a bond with the earth. It was now as if the life within it were streaming up into his body . . . as if he and the earth were living in a silent understanding (*Groei [Growth]*, in *VW* 6:167). Only when both conditions are met—when (a) the good steward who loves his land is (b) forced off the ancestral farm—is faith in natural justice shaken and does the spirit of tragedy enter the *plaasroman*.

The passage above gives rise at once, however, to another question: What is the difference beween love of the farm and love of nature? What are the bounds of the farmer's love? Does his love terminate at the boundaries of the farm? If the farmer owns the farm because he loves it, is it conceivable that he loves the farm only because he owns it? In the passage quoted, it is not only the earth of the ancestral farm that pours its life into Gustav, the *plaasseun* (farmboy) who has shaken the dust of the city off his heels to rediscover himself on the beloved ancestral farm: he loves, and draws strength from, the sky and the clouds too, which belong to all. It is no doubt true that the typically extensive nature of South African farming makes it possible to identify the farm with all that the gaze can embrace, even to think of particular sectors of the sky as belonging to particular farms. Nonetheless, we must note that into the myth of the good farmer and his marriage with his farm are drawn many of the energies of European Romanticism, many of the feelings of cosmic identification and engulfment originally attributed to the relation not of farmer to farm but of man to the wilderness, to forest and moor and mountain. Van den Heever, in *Groei*, is clearly employing a central Romantic theme and adapting it to his own interests: whereas European Romanticism (to simplify for a moment) sees man as a child not of cities but of nature, Van den Heever presents man as a child not of cities but of the farm.

The difference between nature and farm is one which Van den Heever glides over not only in his novels but in his essays. In an essay entitled "The Form of the Afrikaner's Civilization and Culture" he writes that "the slumbering might of the culture of every people" has its basis in "the bondedness of man to the earth." Man is "mystically united . . . by a dark love" to the earth, which is the "soil of generation" of national culture. And in an essay on Stijn Streuvels, a novelist for whom he had unbounded admiration and to whose *De vlaschaard (The Flax-Ground)* (1907) his own novel *Laat vrugte (Late Fruit)* is deeply in debt, he writes of the "dark call of the earth" to be heard in Flemish literature, of the "unconscious love of the soil" and the "love of space, of nature" that can never die in man (*Die Afrikaanse gedagte [The Afrikaans Idea]* 16, 52–53). The love of earth or soil that we read of in Van den Heever's novels is not, however, a variety of love felt by the city-dweller for parkland or by a labourer for the earth he is hired to till, but solely that felt by a man for the earth he owns. Thus self-realization—realization of the self not as individual but, I shall argue below, as the transitory embodiment of a lineage—becomes tied to landownership and to a particular kind of spiritual experience available only to landowners. In consequence Van den Heever writes about the spiritual self-realization of few in South Africa save the Afrikaner. In particular, he writes about an Afrikaner type with roots sunk deep in private land-property, a type that includes all Afrikaners neither in the 1930s nor at any other time in history.[2]

Though the ideal farmer of the *plaasroman* is wedded to the soil of the farm, he is not consciously aware of his married state or becomes aware of it only when it is too late, when he is threatened with losing his farm. Why should this be so? The answer is that the farmer is *natuurmens* (natural man); and once natural man becomes able to articulate his essence in language, he is thereby removed from the realm of nature. Hence the marriage between farmer and farm must remain an unarticulated one, a blood-marriage too deep for words. Yet the paradox is that until this marriage is brought to consciousness the *plaasroman* cannot articulate itself. The craft of the prototypical Van den Heever *plaasroman* must therefore lie in creating the preconditions for an epiphany, an eruption into words, in which for the first time the farm appears to the farmer in the glory of its full meaning, and for the first time the farmer fully knows himself. The movement of the prototypical *plaasroman* is steadily towards the revelation of the farm as a source of meaning. (The city, by contrast, steadfastly refuses to reveal any meaning to the questing pilgrim from the countryside: the implication is that it has none.)

The problematics of consciousness are thus inherent in the *plaasroman,* and Van den Heever's farm novels display a developing engagement with the problem.

II

Op die plaas is the story of Freek, a shy, lonely, impoverished young farmer who falls in love with a town girl. The girl, Miem,

2. On the basis of documentary research, Van der Merwe points out that in or around 1810 fewer than a quarter of "independent farmers" in the Graaff-Reinet district legally owned farms, and that the corresponding figure for Tulbagh lay somewhere beteen 39 percent and 75 percent. He argues for a certain degree of indifference in "the old days" to landownership, not only among poor farmers but among people of means, who would argue that "it was not necessary for a farmer to have his own ground, since one could farm just as well without a farm." This attitude persisted into the twentieth century in corners of the country like Bushmanland, dying out only when nomadic farmers discovered that unless they bought land there would be no more *staanplek* (stopping-place) for them. Van der Merwe 52–55.

flirts with him but passes over him in favour of a wealthier suitor. After a long struggle with hopelessness as well as with a long and dangerous illness, he returns to his farming "newborn," stronger for having survived, ready to forge a new life.[3]

Freek lives by the cycle of the seasons. Thus in spring he feels "vitality"; during his time with Miem love grows in him like a plant; but when she marries, his "fairest life-growth" withers like foliage at the end of summer. He endures a winter of illness. Then, with spring, "joy in life" begins to return, life begins to regenerate itself in his breast: he is a matrix, like the earth, in which the life-force, like a seed, now asserts itself (*OP* 17, 106, 114; *VW* 1:253, 316).

But living in union with the seasons has a second meaning.

> Freek's eye roamed across the landscape, full of new energy, and vitality leapt like a fountain in his heart. It was so vast and so beautiful! Why should he be sad? At this time of year he usually felt better; everywhere life was on the point of budding, and it penetrated him too with soft warmth. Yes, he too was merely a part of nature, part of its cycle; but the seasons came and went and were always changing, only his little life went on [as before]; ... even when he had turned to whitened bones under the cold earth, these same trees, decked in blossoms, would be celebrating another year. [*OP* 17; *VW* 1:253]

To the question "Why should he be sad?" comes the consoling answer: though his individual life may end, the same (generic) trees will continue to be reborn every spring. To the extent that Freek is a temporary home for a transindividual life-force, spring is an occasion for joy; only to the extent that he is an individual manifestation of the life-force is it a memento mori.

An ambivalent response to beauty and vitality is of course a commonplace of Romanticism. In spring an instinctive joie de vivre leaps in Freek's heart; but this is offset by a conscious reflection that all flesh is as grass, that in due course he must die. The "dark impulsivity" (*OP* 74; *VW* 1:290) of his desire to embrace Miem is directed toward continuing his life in the way that the grass and trees continue their lives, by planting their seed;

---

3. *Op die plaas* 116. I quote from the first edition, which was substantially revised for the *Versamelde werke* of 1957.

his failure to press his suit comes from a pessimistic sense of his own worthlessness. He is thus a double being, on the one hand living instinctively in a natural world where living things are not individuals so much as carriers of the germ of their species, on the other hand bearing a melancholy consciousness bound to the life of the individual.

This doubleness poses a clear problem of narration for Van den Heever. Tied to the individual mode of being, consciousness (as long as it is consciousness of individual transitoriness) leads continually to the decline of the hero from activity to the passivity of *weemoed* (melancholy). The problem of creating action thus becomes one of conquering *weemoed* by bringing the protagonist to a supraindividual consciousness, consciousness of himself as a mere manifestation or bearer of the species—or, in the narrower perspective that Van den Heever adopts in his novels, as a manifestation or bearer of the line *(familie)* whose blood runs in his veins. Put differently, the problem is to raise the body-responsiveness which returns *lewenslus* (vitality) to the story, to the level of consciousness. For until he can bring *lewenslus* to consciousness, until his protagonists can utter their vitality for themselves, Van den Heever is doomed to go on acting as their spokesman and interpreter, *telling for* them. Thus, for example: when spring arrives at the end of Faan's sickness, "from every bush outside, from the blue of the sky, from the sunshine, from the soul of nature, there whispered a message of hope" (*OP* 114; cf. *VW* 1:316). Why does the landscape signify hope here when elsewhere it signifies death (*OP* 86; *VW* 1:297)? Might dusk and sunset not have the same signification, or other significations (e.g., peace, the promise of the return of day), or an infinity of significations, or no signification at all? Feeling and being made to feel are, here, ways of reading the landscape. The pessimistic readings belong to consciousness and can be read out by Freek himself. They are, however, as Van den Heever makes clear, the *misreadings* characteristic of individual consciousness. A truer, optimistic reading of the landscape belongs to a lineal consciousness which he, as author, has yet to find a means of articulating. Therefore the truth of the landscape can be expressed only in the form of significations disguised as "feelings" and attached to Freek ("in the dusk he felt something of the greatness of love").

Though *Op die plaas,* an immature and minor work, does not solve the problem of how to bring the lineal self to consciousness, it does try (misdirectedly, I believe) to point to a solution. Freek is not like ordinary people. "He had never had a chance to grow up properly. He had always been a bit of a weakling, and gone his own way." He feels too "poor . . . small . . . weak" to earn Miem's love. He is "shy and sensitive . . . always afraid of life." "The world could never understand him." He is in fact an outsider, an orphan (at least he has no visible family), and a clown (with "soft hat . . . wide jacket . . . and . . . three-quarter trousers . . . pulled up high between his legs") (*OP* 36, 73, 109–10, 6–7; *VW* 1:265, 289, 313–14, 246). His eccentric position in society provides him with the solitude and creates in him the melancholy that turns him into a Romantic reader of nature in the first place; if these first evidences of artistic temperament could only be deepened, we are to infer, Freek would become a reader able to read true meanings. The conquest of grief and illness at the end of the book represents (I think) such a deepening: Freek becomes a "newborn person," still "sensitive" but escaped now from his "idealistic shell" and no longer afraid of life (*OP* 116–17). In other words, while remaining a reader of nature (and thus remaining unlike his farmer neighbours), he is no longer disengaged from life (and thus becomes like them); he is both a reading consciousness and a *natuurmens.* Of how such a representative of lineal consciousness reads the world in practice, however, Van den Heever nevers gives a sample.

Though it is about a farmboy who goes off to the city but then changes his mind and decides that his destiny lies on the farm, and though it does contain readings of nature, *Langs die grootpad (Beside the Road)* (1928) does not engage the problem of the meaning of the farm, which I see as central to the *plaasroman.* Hansie, the dreamy, clumsy farmboy, becomes a promising violinist. Instead of embarking on a career as a performer, however, he returns to the *platteland* (countryside) to marry his childhood sweetheart and help light the "flame of culture" there (fortunately the father with whom he had fallen out has bequeathed him a farm) (178). There is no suggestion that he will ever get his hands dirty: his bride-to-be imagines him spending his days in his study in the farmhouse, composing music. The opposition in *Langs die grootpad* is thus not between city and farm but between city and *platteland;* the Freek figure is diverted into becoming an interpreter of Europe to the Afrikaner rather than remaining an articulator of the experience of the Afrikaner on his farm.

In *Droogte (Drought)* (1930) Van den Heever returns to this earlier theme. The novel presents a range of modes of consciousness formed by the South African landscape. To begin with, we have two, and potentially three, embodiments of individual consciousness so acute that it feels itself to be outside (outside society, outside the nature to which it is nevertheless tied by the fact of mortality). The first of these is the writer of the old diary that falls into the hands of the schoolteacher Hendriks. This diarist, an ancestor of the five brothers who are the main figures in the novel, writes of the veld as "the wilderness." His fellow-colonists, he knows, think him "a fool." He feels that he "was not born for this world," that he is "a castaway on this great world." "My soul spreads its wings, ready to flee into the unending."[4]

What is the nature of the diarist's alienation? It is difficult to read the phrase "this great world *[wêreld]*" as having any other application than to the spaces of Africa. On the other hand, the spirit that wants to flee into the unending seems also to want to escape a social world, perhaps a constricting colonial society (we are given only hints) that finds this schoolteacher-romantic "a fool." Also, the *wêreld* for which he was not born is the world from which he is liberated by the lightning bolt that kills him.

The second representative of the outsider consciousness is Hendriks the schoolteacher himself. Unhappily married to a woman who detests small-town life, he eventually comes to blame his sense of alienation on "the destructive beast of prey, self-analysis," and longs to be *onbewus* (unconscious), as country people are (176–77; *VW* 3:97). He destroys the manuscript of a cher-

---

4. *Droogte* 123–24; *VW* 3:70. Since there are small but significant revisions in the text of the *Versamelde werke,* I cite both editions.

ished essay in praise of the life of the intellect; this act brings about a reconciliation with his wife, and they leave the *platteland* to seek fresh pastures.

Hendriks's one positive achievement is to obtain a bursary for the promising child of one of the pauperized farmer brothers to continue his studies. Though it is not clear how this child will achieve education and yet evade the teeth of the "beast of prey, self-analysis," the implication of the ending of the novel (an upbeat ending characteristic of Van den Heever) is that he is to escape both the social fate of *armblankedom* (poor white status), into which his parents have fallen, and the spiritual fate of alienation. In this respect he is to be like Hansie in *Langs die grootpad,* though, without a farm to inherit, it is unclear what social role he can play but that of teacher and yearner after farm life ("that unconscious *[onbewuste]* love of the earth that is to be felt clearly only once one has to part from the farm," as Van den Heever puts it in *Die Afrikaanse gedagte* 52).

All three of these figures are, however, peripheral to the main action of the novel, which concerns the great drought, the efforts of Sagrys to use the drought to squeeze his brothers off their land, and the vengeance of nature upon him. The true, the trustworthy vehicle of consciousness in the novel is not Hendriks but Soois, the brother who ascends from *onbewustheid* (unconsciousness) to a position from which he can understand and interpret the story of the brothers. Hendriks and the diarist ancestor are in the book to represent, however sketchily, an alienated mode of response to the natural world. Soois is not alienated; nevertheless, he cannot articulate his unalienated self as long as he remains *onbewus.* Van den Heever thus finds himself in the same impasse as in *Op die plaas.* He escapes it by a trick: he asserts the growth of Soois from blindness (impoverishment and aridity of insight during the time of drought) to illumination (after the drought is broken) by asserting a real (not metaphoric) bond between this growth and the cycle of nature (from drought to rains), and by claiming that to be brought to illumination by the order of nature is to escape the slough into which Hendriks has fallen and attain a form of natural consciousness.

This latter assertion is a significant one. For to claim that consciousness is at one with the natural cycle of drought and rain is to claim that meanings can be read out from nature without the medium of a code, that nature is a system of symbols with which a certain kind of consciousness (natural consciousness) is inherently in tune. Soois virtually asserts this thesis: "Is there not a great lesson hidden in life, a lesson that each of us has to learn through hardship?" (212; *VW* 3:116). Van den Heever thus solves his problem—the problem of representing natural consciousness in the novel—by denying the necessity of a language with the function of mediating between nature and meaning: nature *is* meaning, drought *is* blindness. The arbitrariness of such correspondences is a measure of the arbitrariness of the solution.

That Van den Heever was seriously concerned with representing prereflective consciousness in *Droogte* is indicated by the presence of Datie, the deaf-mute imbecile brother who, acting in some sense as the agent of the justice of the universe, kills Sagrys. In early scenes of the novel, hunting hares with stones, spending his days in the shade of a bush, Datie is no more than an animal. The angry kick that Sagrys gives him, however, has the effect of translating him from an unreflecting animal consciousness to a lonely animal consciousness, if such a state is possible (Van den Heever anyway attributes it to him—Datie feels like "an animal abandoned to its fate here in the drought-thinned endlessness of the veld" [46; *VW* 3:31]), and from there to a true alienated human consciousness: he experiences "a terrible loneliness," feels that "he is nowhere needed, is a burden on the world" (47; *VW* 3:31). The vengeance of Datie of course stands for the vengeance of the natural order on Sagrys for all his unnatural, unfilial acts—the dispossession of his brothers as well as the kicking of Datie and the use of him in general "as a *hotnot* [Hottentot]" (74; "as a serf" *VW* 3:45)—and thus (again) for the thesis that events constitute a natural language (Soois's "lesson"); nevertheless, the relentless hatred Datie comes to feel for Sagrys is a consequence of his newborn consciousness of himself as a creature alone in the landscape.

Datie is not the only idiot-figure in the *plaasroman:* one thinks as well of Faan in D. F. Malherbe's *Die meulenaar (The Miller)*

(1926) and of Jochem van Bruggen's Ampie. The idiot represents a form of consciousness that does not question the meaning of experience, and hence does not feel the *weemoed* (melancholy) that Van den Heever and Malherbe, in different ways, associate with reflectiveness (whether Ampie can truly be called an idiot after the opening pages of Van Bruggen's trilogy is another question). The most elementary trouble with the idiot as a protagonist for the *plaasroman* is, however, that for eugenic reasons he may not marry (this is the veiled subject of *Die meulenaar*). Thus though he may represent a way of living wholly at one with the natural world, he cannot represent an answer to the question of what kind of consciousness is appropriate to the farm, where the continuity of the marriage between farm and lineage requires that the farmer have not only parents but children.

Groei (1933) is much more of a *roman à thèse* than the earlier works, both in its social thinking and in confronting the problem of consciousness lying at the heart of the kind of novel Van den Heever wants to write. Its central protagonist, Gustav Cloete, faces a choice: whether to stay on in the city (where he has lost his job as a journalist and has been able to find work only in the railway workshops) or return to the family farm, which is on its last legs as a result of the drought and low prices. His years among city people, including urbanized Afrikaners, have proved to him that the city offers nothing but insidious moral corruption and contemptible material values. The farm, on the contrary, stands not only for an integration of self and nature that he remembers from his childhood, but for a kind of work of more indubitable value than anything he can do in the city.

The thesis of *Groei* is thus that farm life is in all senses better than city life, and that the Afrikaner betrays himself when he quits the land. "This earth has kept its people *[volk]* what they are," says Gustav's father; in the cities the Afrikaner will simply *versleg* (degenerate) (*VW* 6:71). And though Gustav's brother argues that the Afrikaner is being driven off the land by forces beyond his control, including the shrinking of farms to an uneconomic size, the case histories that Gustav considers, including those of his father-in-law and his brother, provide more evidence of rash speculation, reckless spending, and idleness than of ineluctable fate. Thus—although it does not push the case hard—*Groei* does seem to advance a return to the farm as a general salvation for the deracinated urban Afrikaner rather than as simply a retreat for a minority of sensitive souls. Put otherwise, there is nothing in the book to contradict the reading that every *plaasseun* who is prepared to work hard and live frugally can make a living on the ancestral farm (since Gustav and his brother work the farm jointly, the problem of the fragmenting of farmland via multiple inheritance is evaded).

The energy of Van den Heever's writing in *Groei* goes into the exploration of the inner processes that lead Gustav first to recover his true self on the farm and then to lose himself in work for (rather than on) the farm. Summoned to his father's deathbed, he wanders around the farm for days feeling that "the wires of his development had got mixed up" (a revealingly mechanistic image for his self-conception at this initial stage). Then, in the "great peace" of the veld, he sits down beside a stream and with "dreamstruck eyes" falls into a reverie about the meaning of existence and of individual suffering. He can see no goal to life, only "a dark absence of reason . . . a blind fate." As he sits "a flock of doves . . . coasted rhythmically overhead, swam elegantly in circles, and disappeared over the bulge of the hill." As if liberated from the halls of memory by the flight of the doves, lines of verse begin to ascend to consciousness in Gustav. In stately rhythms the verses tell him to undergo "the suffering allotted him," for in accepting it he will find "brotherhood of peace in suffering." Taking heart from the lesson that "man is great only when he is unconquerable," Gustav discovers that he is now ready to confront life again. Hereafter he daily returns to the veld where he experienced this illumination, every day yielding "deeper and surer insight" (158–60, 162).

What is important here is not the content of the advice the verses give but the fact that the answer to Gustav's questionings, long hidden within him, emerges under the maieutic guidance of the circling doves in the great peace of the veld. It is *as if* nature speaks to Gustav, using the words that lie hidden in him because nature has no words of its own (Van den Heever at this point abandons the natural language on which he has hitherto relied to carry the message of illumination). His principle of construction, here as in the earlier novels, however, still consists in laying the groundwork for, and building up towards, these moments of stillness and intensity in which the truth comes to the subject. Such moments of truth are of course the raison d'être of Romantic nature poetry, occurring as Wordsworthian "spots of time" in the life of the soul. The art of such Romantic poetry, like Van den Heever's art, is one of rhetorically fortifying the moment of vision so that the message spoken through the subject will seem to come not from his untrustworthy civilized self but from the voice of nature speaking through him.

It might seem that the goal of Van den Heever's strategy is merely to naturalize certain moral dicta—for example, the dictum that suffering creates brotherhood—thereby lending them the prestige of a natural origin. However, what is important is not so much *what* nature leads the subject to utter—it is usually a platitude—as *that* nature has brought him to the moment of utterance. Because the words emerge from him "naturally," he cannot doubt them; nor may anyone else, including the reader. Thus the spots of time constituted by these insights become islands of certainty in the story, their certainty being not so much their content as the newfound self-certainty they mark in the questing subject. To attain such an island of truth in the narrative means that the subject will be understood to act henceforth on the basis of his own truth. The subject therefore becomes an exemplar of man in a state of integration; whatever Gustav proceeds to do, acting upon the message liberated in him by the doves, will be marked as truthful.

(In novels written within this Romantic epistemology—one may note—a pair of characters in conflict, and on whose conflict the action turns, are rarely, perhaps never, *both* allowed communion with nature, since if that were permitted we would have a conflict in which the two sides not only believed in their own right but in terms of the epistemology were both right.)

Nothing in Gustav's communing with nature thus far distinguishes farm from nature: doves fly where they will, after all, acknowledging no boundaries. But the veld in which Gustav wanders is privileged ground, being the ground of his childhood. The implication of the fact that he has to return to this part of the world and wander in this veld before he recovers himself is that he could not have found himself elsewhere. Furthermore, Gustav's return is connected with the approaching death of his father and therefore with the destiny of the ancestral farm. Though his father grows weaker every day,

> upon the whole farm the work of [his] sturdy personality was to be seen. . . . Since [Gustav] had departed the farm, it had been just as if his father had departed from his life, and yet it was not so, for in the background of his entire spiritual life the great figure had stood. . . . And now at this turning-point in his life his father stepped fully into the light, and with the power of his personality acted creatively upon the future development of his son. [162–63]

This passage is significant. As his real-life father literally wastes away, the figure of the father, farmer and patriarch, hitherto hidden within Gustav, begins to emerge into consciousness. At the same time, the traces of the history of his father's labour on the face of the earth begin to emerge into clarity, and moments of communion with nature on the farm cause the hitherto hidden truth to emerge from Gustav. At all levels there is a *vergestaltiging* (a taking on of form, an emergence of truth). In the same way that communion with the farm as nature leads Gustav to the truth (or to being filled with truth), so a vision of the farm as a part of nature on which a history of labour is inscribed leads that figure in Gustav which looms larger as his biological father dwindles—a transindividual figure standing for the line of patriarchal farmer-fathers—to utter a second truth, a truth again of less importance in itself than as a talisman to prove that action based upon it will be truthful action. Gustav falls asleep in the veld. While he sleeps, his father leaves this life but bequeaths a last commandment: "Keep the farm" (166).

The rhetorical force of the last pages of *Groei* may blind the reader to Van den Heever's strategy, which is sometimes to use farm and nature as opposing concepts, sometimes to identify them, in the interest of a single, overriding purpose. Nature is presented in images of sky, grass and bushes, birds and insects, streams; by getting out into this environment, from which evidences of human work are absent and where perspectives are infinite (no fences are visible), Gustav is able to rediscover his true self. But to actualize that self he has to yield up his individuality in a devotion of labour to the past and future of the farm, which is nature inscribed with fences, walls, buildings, boreholes, irrigation channels, and signed above all with the scars of the plough. Gustav guides the ploughshare: "Never yet had Gustav felt such a bond with the earth. It was . . . as if the life within it were streaming up into his body . . . as if he and the earth were living in a silent understanding. . . . He felt at one with sky, clouds and soil." The smell of turned soil fills him with "a dizzying love of the earth . . . for which his fathers had had such a mysterious love, a love that had once been incomprehensible to him" (167). From one point of view it is the farm that has finally allowed Gustav to become a man of nature, to recover his nature. Through the element of earth, which here becomes the key factor in common between farm and nature, Gustav grows at one with the cosmos ("sky, clouds and soil") at the same time that he is drawn into the mystic marriage between his lineage and the farm. From another point of view, however, it is nature that has allowed Gustav to become a man of the farm: the full weight of the Romantic tradition that makes nature the source of truth has been thrown behind Gustav to validate his self-assertion as a farmer ploughing his own ground, his own patch of earth.

Van den Heever's will to see farm and nature as one occasions certain deformations of the reality of farming life. Because the prime characteristic of nature as Van den Heever writes of it is spaciousness, there is little emphasis on limits (fences) and therefore on society (neighbours); indeed, what irritates his farmers (farmers by nature) when they go to the city is above all the lack of space, in both physical and social senses, and hence the feeling of being hemmed in, of becoming small (petty), of not having room in which the spirit can grow. Furthermore, to the extent that Van den Heever's writing represents farming as a heroic activity that transports the subject into the mythic time of the ancestors, workaday operations like the management of farm labour and the keeping of accounts get pushed into the background in favour of timeless (because seasonal and recurrent) activities like ploughing and reaping. Even animal husbandry (which in real life involves incessant accounting) is slighted by comparison with intensive agriculture. Given his particular point of view, it is not hard to understand Van den Heever's dissatisfaction with the novels of Abraham Jonker, whose picture of farm life is dominated by accounting, stock management, scheming over landownership, etc.: "The earth is inadequately depicted [in Jonker]," Van den Heever complains. "The writer . . . does not depict the limitless plains" (*Die Afrikaanse gedagte* 107).

One of the elements of the earth-myth not employed in *Groei* is the figure of the earth as repository for the bones of the ancestors. This element is added in *Somer* (1935). The relation of the Du Preez brothers to nature and farm, and hence to their ancestors, emerges in the following passage:

> Through their bodies, their souls, nature worked, worked in seasons. . . . So they continued, ever shrouded in an atmosphere that kept changing mysteriously from season to season, and in their eyes they bore the melancholy of life that arises and perishes . . . , in their hearts dark knowledge of the life working through them, knowledge of the force of the seasons that go on with ineluctable certainty till the end of all acts of creation . . . and over the goal of it all, God disposed. [161]

Here, side by side, are the two kinds of awareness characteristic of Van den Heever's *plaasroman:* on the one hand a *weemoed*-filled awareness that all flesh is as grass, on the other a "dark knowledge" that what in *Groei* was called "die lewenskern" (the life-kernel) is greater than the individual, who merely acts as carrier for it. Limited to the first kind of consciousness, the subject is threatened with paralysis in the face of the question of the meaning of it all; the argument of *Somer,* like that of the earlier *plaasromans,* is carried on on behalf of the second, "dark" consciousness, through which the lineage and perhaps the race as well speak.

It is on the side of this "dark knowledge" that the voices of the ancestors are brought into the novel. "Over there at the churchyard," says Tom, "it felt as if someone were telling me that Great-grandfather, Grandfather, Father and all the others would be shamed if we let the ground go." The "as if" marks the step in Van den Heever's narrative logic where he is driven to analogy (here), as he is driven to dream (in *Groei*) or vision (in *Laat vrugte*), to achieve the transition from individual consciousness (here Tom's consciousness) to lineal consciousness. At the heart of each of Van den Heever's exercises in the *plaasroman* lies the problem of finding novelistic means of making the transition. In more than one sense, the attainment of lineal consciousness in the *plaasroman* becomes like the consummation of true love in the novel of marriage: the achievement not only of the blending of the questing subject with the beloved, but also of the end of the discontent of individual consciousness, thus bringing the novel to its proper end. The problem of consciousness, for the *plaasroman* as for the novel of marriage, is therefore bound up with the problem of attaining the right ending.

Laat vrugte (1939) is distinguished from the earlier farm novels in having a central character who actively resists evolution from individual to lineal consciousness. Sybrand treats the cycle of the seasons, the march of generations, not as a fate to be contemplated with *weemoed* but as an unacceptable destiny to be struggled against with might and main, "as if it were something great and godless that one's own blood [specifically his son Henning] should survive to rule over the heritage of the [fore]fathers" (35). In effect Sybrand wants to live forever, wants the line to come to stasis in his person. The sights and sounds of spring that had filled earlier protagonists with a sense of transitoriness fill him with, if anything, vigour; the sound of the wind in the trees is like "a hymn of nature to his own creative power" (251).

Sybrand's mother exhibits the same spirit. Bequeathed life-long usufruct over the farm, she exercises her rights mercilessly to claim half of whatever the farm produces. She justifies her refusal to yield up parental authority over a middle-aged son on the grounds that parents who treat their children mildly make them idle and useless and "not careful enough of what they have inherited." This lesson of harshness she learned from her own parents, but its ultimate origin is attributed to the pioneer ancestors: "For people who had to clear stretches of bush, build endless *kraal*-walls, plant stone fenceposts . . . , there was no time for . . . softness" (38).

While both Sybrand and his mother are plainly rationalizing, that is, adducing arguments to conform to their will, in neither case is the motive one of material greed. Sybrand treats not only his son (whom he effectively drives off the farm) but his brother-in-law and his daughter in an unfamilial way. He turns his wife into a house-servant. But, like his mother, he is able to justify autocracy on the grounds of duty to the farm and the ancestors who built it up (45, 139). He and his mother see themselves as, in each case, the repository of the true values of the ancestors, and see everyone else as *pap* (soft). The virtues which, in their eyes, they possess and their successors lack are hardness and industry. Their great fear is that the farm will fall into the hands of lazy people who will *boer agteruit* (lose ground).

It is easy enough to read *Laat vrugte* as a didactic exercise, to say that its subject is *hardkoppigheid* (stubbornness) and that by the time Sybrand finally accepts his error, passes the reins to his son, and dies, we have been subjected to a lesson in generational relations. But, read as a lesson, the novel is of little interest. It is built into the structure of succession in the landowning class that there should be a period of strife between father and son while both are living on the familial estate and each feels that the other is too young or too old to govern it. It is also inevitable that the father should be defeated (because he is on the wane) and the son triumph (because he is young). The question is therefore not *what* Sybrand learns about life but *why* it is that he comes to a state of illumination about life—in other words, *how* it is that the novel comes to be meaningful.

Whereas, when the ancestors were present in the earlier novels, they were present as, at most, a force speaking through the blood-consciousness of the living, in *Laat vrugte* they have their own ghostly existence. For example: Sybrand, his wife, and son sit around the supper table. Among them occurs "a moment of coming to consciousness," and in the shadows they feel the propinquity of

a super-personal sphere in which past generations tried to express their exhausted [*uitgeleefd*, lived-out] existence, in which
day and night long gone, hours of hard work, petty plans and
vanity and bitter feuds long forgotten, once more became reality, and the departed felt themselves bound tightly to those
who now sat in their places. [84]

We are a far cry here from the sturdy ancestors of *Somer* urging
from their graves that the farm be held on to. These are spirits
who cannot let go of life, who want to live through their flesh-
and-blood descendants, trying to attain through them what they
failed to attain in their own lives. To comprehend the kind of
prior existence these shades had in their day we need look no
further than Sybrand's wife, Betta, who feels that she is "slowly
dying," her life's dreams trampled, "pushed away downward,
lower, to the earth," particularly her dream of escaping "things
immovable, fixed, forever still, mortared together, like her own
life" (81, 72). And, like the dead *(dodes)* of the supper scene,
Betta does indeed return after her death "a being with the super-
human might of the dead, with the unearthly power to terrify
that belonged to a spirit trampled down in life . . . [in search of]
recovery, compensation, revenge [where she] had been turned
into a serf" (268). Thus a different explanation emerges in this
case for why the ancestors do not want the farm to leave the
hands of the family: because it is only vicariously, through the
lives of their descendants, that they can hope to realize the aspira-
tions which the "hard work, petty plans and vanity and bitter
feuds" of their lives had not yielded.

What does this all mean? Inheritance seems to lie as a virtual
curse on Sybrand's family line. Each generation must labour to
make up for the spiritual failure of its predecessors. There is no
talk of a transcendent duty to the soil. Has Van den Heever
made an about-face?

Not if we take into consideration the kind of family Van den
Heever describes here. The attitude toward the farm expressed
by Sybrand and his mother is quite different from that of Gustav
in *Groei*. In particular, they do not conceive of the farm as nature
at all. It is certainly more than a mere economic resource; but
what appears to have passed them by (Van den Heever does not

articulate this lack, one has to infer it) is the experience of surrender to the cosmos and the consequent loss of self that would
make the later surrender of *lewenskrag* (life-force) so much less
annihilating. Having lived with their noses close to the ground,
Sybrand and his mother lack the expansion of spirit that comes
with a sense of the space of the farm. *Laat vrugte* has a more
European feel than the earlier novels: Sybrand is much like one
of the rich peasants of Balzac or Streuvels.

The spirits of the ancestors do more, however, than pin the
living down on the ancestral farm. They also call the living to them
when it is time for the living to depart, and protect the farm
against outsiders. Thus when Sybrand's mother approaches
death, "it was as if those who had lived here before . . . wanted to
speak to her, to call her, more intimately than ever, because she
was now shuffling nearer and nearer to their dead land." Buried,
she lies "next to her husband, among generations that had long
ago been carried in here and were waiting patiently for the blood
of their blood" (108, 113). When Sybrand marries a second time,
marrying Maggie, the widow of a former *bywoner*, a woman who
schemes to inherit the farm and dispossess his son, the spirits
intervene. In the following passage it is not clear whether we have
authorial narration or Maggie's *style indirect libre*—whether the
dead are authorially asserted to be haunting her or whether she
merely imagines them. No doubt the ambiguity is intentional.

> The dead of [the farm] Boskloof who had laboured here with-
> out cease, whose handiwork stood all around, whose bodies
> were intergrown with the soil of the farm, shuffled invisible
> through this house, they were about on the farm, they wanted
> to preserve it for their blood, they wanted continuity, they
> wanted to endure in their descendants. [302]

Maggie feels that

> the heavy stillness of the farm lay like a motionless reptile on
> her thoughts, and would slowly drive her to madness. The
> great farm-stillness in which these people had lived in safety,
> was outside her, awoke fear in her. She was the intruder who
> would have to give herself over entirely to the forming forces
> at work here, or else flee. [316]

The silence of the farm has come to be associated no longer with the silence of nature but with the silence of the living dead. The dead want continuity, not because (as happens to be the case) the son is a "good" heir and the new wife a "bad" one but because a takeover of the farm by a line of intruders (Maggie already has a lover) will mean the end of their vicarious life.

And when the usurper is expelled and Henning returns to the farm, bringing with him the grandson who will inherit it in turn, Sybrand, dying, feels in the clasp of his son's hand that "he had touched the generations to come" and that "he would after all be reborn *[herlewe]* in the generations that issued from him" (334). Thus the ancestors—already on the point of including Sybrand in their ranks—triumph, though no longer maleficently.

Laat vrugte is not a book about a haunted farm but a book that uses—perhaps too literally—the metaphor of haunting to consolidate a set of related mythic ideas: (1) that a family is capable of owning a farm in a supralegal way; (2) that this right is attained through a history of labour invested in the farm by a line of ancestors; (3) that the living family, owing a duty to the ancestors who lie buried there, must remain on, and therefore in a certain sense belongs on, the farm. These three ideas have already been seen at work in Van den Heever's novels. What is new, however, is: (4) that the unfulfilled nature of their lives, the pettiness of their toil, gives rise to a tyranny of the unsleeping dead over the living. This fourth idea, which is profoundly at odds with the theme of *Arbeitsfreude* that runs through the *plaasroman* and is at the centre of *Groei,* is not contradicted by the life history of Sybrand himself, though overtly the last pages of the book say that Sybrand is relinquishing his hold on the farm and on his descendants, and therefore will not join the ranks of the ghosts. For Sybrand's life, however materially successful, has been characterized, till the time of his incapacitating stroke, by precisely the "hours of hard toil, petty plans and vanity and bitter feuds" that rendered the lives of his ancestors unfulfilling.

If (as the novel seems to say) Sybrand will not haunt Henning, what is it that brings about his redemption from the *ewige Wiederkehr?* All we know is that, after his disillusioning second marriage, he begins to have doubts about the life he has lived. He seeks reconciliation with his neighbour and begins to feel an "obscure pride" in Henning for having had the courage "to obey and honour the deep fulfilment for which life ever seeks," even though this has entailed revolt against his father. Sybrand seeks "understanding of his [own] deeds" and slowly begins to gain "new wisdom, insight that is only won through experience" (308, 309). After the stroke he has "moments of unnatural clarification" in which he has visions of his deceased first wife as she was when once he loved her (322)—that is to say, he experiences the return of one of the dead in a benign aspect. But whether this sketchy spiritual evolution within Sybrand adds up to enough to create a break between the living and the dead, and thus end the haunting, is to be doubted. What is absent from the story is the transfiguring experience present in the earlier books, an experience that belongs to the temple of the farm-as-nature. The trouble with inserting it, however (if we can imagine such an episode inserted), is that if transfiguring experience were accessible to Sybrand, one might wonder why it was not accessible to his ancestors, who after all lived on the same holy ground. The attempt to bring the ancestors into greater prominence in *Laat vrugte,* whatever somber power it has lent the novel, has also brought into prominence questions about the ancestors which Van den Heever does not face, the chief of them a simple ethical question: when the farmer justifies his transcendent right to own the farm on the grounds of a duty to *voor-* and *nageslagte* (generations before and after) is he not simply substituting for the selfishness of one the selfishness of the lineage? It would seem that the purely psychological mode of *Laat vrugte* (if we do Van den Heever the credit of conceiving of his ghosts as figures in the awareness of his protagonists) is not adequate to the ultimate purpose of the *plaasroman,* namely, to provide transcendental justification for ownership of the land. The religious energies incorporated in Romantic myths of communion with nature seem to be required as well.

Laat vrugte is not, in fact, a novel about nature at all, in the sense that *Groei* is. There is no ecstatic experience of the natural world, no experience of the yielding up of the self. Much of what experience of nature there is, tends to be of an alien world: one thinks not only of Maggie's experience of the "heavy farm stillness" but of Johanna's experience of the "heavy veld stillness," of shadows lying "motionless and strange" on the ground: "Everything had . . . taken on the overwhelming form of [this] motionlessness, the sun, the air, overarching space and the things that lived in it" (159). Sybrand's heart leaps when he hears the dance of the wind in the poplars. He hears it as "a hymn of nature to his creative power"; but in truth it is only the rustling of leaves misheard, misinterpreted.

Gister (Yesterday) (1941) is Van den Heever's last farm novel. Ouma (Grandma) lives on Vyffontein, forty-five hundred acres of land yielding the barest subsistence to six grown children and their families. Persuaded to sell the farm by a favourite grandson, the plausible cheat Fransie, she accompanies the family to Fordsburg and the life of *armblankes* (poor whites). After the passage of years during which her children and grandchildren are either beaten down by hardship or subtly corrupted, Ouma takes the body of Fransie (killed in an accident) back to the farm, to die within sight of the beloved, lost land.

The theme of *Gister* is the corrupting power of city life. It explores the nature of the link between family and farm no more than cursorily.[5] Only in clarifying the opposition between the respective experiences of space in the city and on the farm—an opposition between constriction and expansion of the spirit—does *Gister* go further than the earlier farm novels.

"Daiel se afskeid" ("Daiel's Farewell") (1945)[6] is the story of an inarticulate sheepshearer who saves enough money to buy a small farm and get married. His farming prospers; but he undergoes a series of inexplicable and uncontrollable fits of violence that persuade him to give up a settled life and return to a life of solitary wandering. The fits of violence—unleashed mainly against his wife—signify, one must suppose, a release of unacknowledged aggression against the family that long ago abandoned him to an orphanage, as well as a way of magically controlling the threat of being abandoned a second time by provoking that abandonment,

5. The furthest the exploration is taken is when Ouma remembers her late husband's advice to her never to sell the farm, "for in their souls they bore that farm, through being linked with it they had become one" (369).

6. In *Kringloop van die winde,* in *VW* 2:7–85.

and reveal Van den Heever working in a clearly psychological mode. Within the mythology of the *plaasroman* the story is also about the persistence of the past: Daiel, who has inherited nothing, neither land nor money nor brains nor words, sets about becoming a landowner and founding his own dynasty but discovers that there remain the forefathers to contend with—in this case not the spirits of the farm but the spirits within lineal memory. Daiel is thus doomed (the story is above all about doom) not to inherit, but to become a wanderer-figure like Wynand in *Somer* and the diarist in *Droogte:* people who, in the absence of a class of farmer-mystics, generate an immense weight of meaning on behalf of the farm by at the same time yearning for it and being held at a distance from it.

III

In the conceptual scheme of Van den Heever's farm novels there are thus two realms: on the one hand city and town, on the other nature and farm. The relation between nature and farm is complex. City and town can, however, be assimilated as places where the limiting horizon and the pressure of human society constrict the soul and prevent its growth.

On the farm are people at various stages of spiritual growth. There are those wrapped in the business of profit and loss, or in plans for extending their empire, who might as well be in the city (Sagrys in *Droogte*, Faan in *Somer*). There are those who refuse to look up from the unceasing round of labour to face the fact of their mortality (the early Sybrand in *Laat vrugte*). Then there are ordinary people who, because they live close to nature, are touched on occasion with yearning and *weemoed*, drawn out of themselves by sky, sunsets, wide horizons, and other spacious perspectives. In some cases this is an inarticulate longing (a longing that has to be expressed for the protagonist via authorial intervention) to expand beyond spatial and temporal limitations (Freek in *Op die plaas*, Wynand and Tom in *Somer*), in others (the diarist in *Droogte*, Gustav in *Groei*) the protagonist is himself a man of words capable of explaining the mood as originating in an awareness of being doomed to die while the world lives on.

Then there are those who transcend *weemoed:* Freek by the end of *Op die plaas,* Soois by the end of *Droogte,* Gustav by the end of *Groei,* Sybrand by the end of *Laat vrugte.* Generally speaking, such transcendence is attained via conscious acceptance that the unit of life is the lineage, not the individual. The attainment of lineal consciousness is brought about by, and brings about, a new relation to nature which in turn clarifies the meaning of the farm. The manifestation of the lineage in historical time is the farm, an area of nature inscribed with the signs of the lineage: with evidences of labour and with bones in the earth (here I pass over the status of the presences in *Laat vrugte*). Lineal consciousness brings about a liberation from the sense of being alone in the world and doomed to die: as long as the lineage lasts the self may be thought to last. Conversely, the self may perpetuate itself by perpetuating the lineage, something that can be done only on the farm because the city is a place where the line gets lost (the family members go their own ways), as in *Gister.* One can maintain the lineage on the farm, however, only as long as the farm prospers. The farmer must *boer vooruit,* while at the same time, by maintaining the infinite perspective that gazes past and beyond all boundaries, he lives on the farm as in nature.

In the scheme of persons I have sketched, there is one hiatus. Where is the representative of Wordsworth's shepherd, a person unreflectively at one with nature, feeling no *weemoed* when the sun sets, not yet at a stage of evolution at which he is afflicted with individual consciousness? This figure is represented only by Datie in *Droogte,* at the stage before he is kicked into loneliness, and perhaps by Daiel, who, however, discovers that his consciousness is not as empty as he thought, being peopled with ghosts. From one point of view, one might recognize that novels cannot be written about simplicity that remains simplicity, and that, though the Van den Heever hero must be ushered towards prereflective consciousness, such consciousness comes only after the struggle of transcending a false individual consciousness. From another point of view, we might want to connect the virtual absence of prereflective consciousness in Van den Heever with the absence from his world of a representation of the consciousness of the figure that has traditionally, in Romantic art, stood for that state of being: the savage, the black man as man of nature.[7]

As for the treatment of nature, Van den Heever is broadly concerned to integrate nature into the farm, that is to say, to relate certain Romantic commonplaces about the recovery of man's truth in nature to the thesis that the Afrikaner will lose his independence and (eventually) his identity if he loses his base in landownership. Since this is the point at which Van den Heever's political thinking and his metaphysics come together—or are brought together, forcibly, under the urgent historical pressures of the 1930s—let me isolate and retrace the development of the *ideology of the farm* in his novels.

In *Op die plaas* the farm itself is not of central ideological importance, in that Freek might as well be a plain countryman as a landed proprietor. Nevertheless, to Van den Heever one must be at least a countryman to read nature: the city-born, lost to their roots, cannot do it, nor can the country-born move to the city and read nature from memory. Memory will not suffice because of the character taken on by the moment of illumination in Van den Heever: a kinaesthetic motion of expansion of the body in the presence of extended perspectives, a motion that draws the soul along in ecstatic illumination.[8] In fact, in *Droogte* the reason why Soois reads nature not as a book open before his eyes but rather in memory, specifically posing the interpretation of the drought as a problem of allegory ("Might there not be a great lesson hidden in life?"), may well be that the allegorical message in question (that the drought mirrors inner aridity, that it is a divine testing) is not compatible with the movement of

7. There is a brief entry into the consciousness of the black farmhand Molief in "Daiel se afskeid"; but during this moment Molief thinks only of his attitude toward Daiel (45–46).

8. This moment is also represented in Van den Heever's poetry of the 1930s. Two examples, from poems in *Aardse vlam*, 1938 (*Versamelde gedigte* 158, 183), are: "O verre wydtes van die groot-oop dag, / my siel vloei na die wasige vertes in." [O far breadths of the vast-open day, / my soul flows out into the hazy distances.] "O laat my wegruis in die wit verskuiming van jou toppe / en uitgaan met jou trekkende gety / na blou, verskuiwende horisonne . . ." [O let me whisper away in the white foaming of your [wave]tops / and go out with the tug of your tide / to blue, shifting horizons . . .]

ecstatic expansion. Therefore the moment of expansion, obligatory in Van den Heever as a seal of validation that the insight arrived at is true, blest, is shifted to the last sentence of the novel as a form of guarantee that the end attained is a true end.

Groei is the novel in which the legacy of Romantic nature-poetry is most clearly used in service of the ideology of the farm. In the major moment of ecstatic illumination, Gustav perceives that what his life lacks is rootedness: the image of a truly lived life is provided by a tree, which because it is rooted can afford to stretch upward to the "wide endlessnesses." In his moment of illumination Gustav feels "as if his soul were expanding, mighty and great," and at the same time experiences an "urge to toil." The link between ecstatic experience and labour, that is to say, between the feeling of spatial unboundedness and farming, is maintained throughout the last pages of the book. Spring on the farm is presented in metaphors of work and power (the "mighty creative work" of the sun) and of natural dynamism (grass ripples, leaves stir, branches sway, colours flame). In this environment the "intense power of labouring *[arbeidskrag]*" that Gustav and his brother feel seems entirely appropriate; and the ecstasy of labour, an expansion of personal energy over the face of the land and a yielding to the "life-urge," takes the subject back in a circle to the experience of "endlessness" (165–67).

By comparison with *Groei, Somer*—Van den Heever's best-known novel—is a work of lesser ideological ambition. Although it portrays human activity under the sign of summer and the cycle of the seasons, and although there are the customary responses of *weemoed* to the infinitudes of time and space, the link between the experience of nature and questions of landownership remains cursory. The farmer-brothers resolve to stay on the land out of piety to the ancestors, out of newfound determination, because town life would be too miserable; there is no transcendent experience to validate their decision.

Laat vrugte, on the other hand, conveys both a more equivocal presentation of nature (which is sometimes unsettling and alien) and a greater attention to the psychology of illumination. When enlightenment comes to Sybrand, it comes not as a blinding experience of full knowledge but as passing moments of clarity when "wisdom" appears on the horizon of awareness. It is not until the last page, and then in muted form, that he reconciles himself to the "eternal laws" that decree that he will die though his line will continue on the farm. Thus the final effect of *Laat vrugte* is to qualify the impression left by *Groei* that farming in South Africa is an activity carried on by an elect class in communion with the cosmos.

The farm, as constituted in Van den Heever's ideology, partakes of the metaphysical and the geographical, of desire and reality. Because it is not solely engendered by desire, the utopian vision of a nation of farming families regenerating themselves endlessly out of the earth is necessarily qualified by geographical reality (there is a limit to the land) as well as by a looming historical reality (the drift of the Afrikaner to the cities continues unabated through the 1930s). Thus it is not surprising that an ideological vision presented so triumphantly in 1933 should grow muted by the end of the decade.

IV

It is a commonplace of criticism of Van den Heever that his fiction moves uneasily between "romanticism" and "realism." In *Droogte,* write Gerhard J. Beukes and Felix V. Lategan, Van den Heever's affiliations to romanticism, the "symbolist nature of his vision," constitute an obstacle to a "noble *[groots]* objectively realistic representation" of the great drought in South Africa and the farmer's "heroic struggle" against it. In *Somer,* they go on, he fails to depict the natural world as "uplifting *reality in and of itself,*" instead allowing it to become "a means of expression for the artist's sense of life" (222, 224). Ernst van Heerden finds a "romantic-realistic dualism" at the core of Van den Heever's art (Nienaber 336); J. C. Kannemeyer concurs, writing of Van den Heever's "hesitation . . . between realism and romanticism" (1:298). In a biographical essay, S. C. Hattingh suggests that Van den Heever turned to writing as an "escape" from the banal reality of "ordinary farm work" (Nienaber 70).

The notion that as a novelist Van den Heever was working in a medium to which he was not temperamentally suited, or to which he could not commit himself wholeheartedly, or whose generic demands he could not satisfy, is tempting but facile, betraying a failure to grasp the scale of the problem confronting him, as it confronts all writers trying to move from a stage of "objectively realistic representation" to a stage of reading the significations that lie behind or within reality, so that reality will not merely be itself but become an *order of significations* (in Abel Coetzee's term, "die natuurwetlikheid," the order of natural law [126]) and yield a structure of meaning. The broad solution tried out by Van den Heever comes from the repertoire of solutions provided by Romanticism: to divide the world of the real into a realm possessed of significance (nature, the country, the farm) and a realm of chaos (the city), to link the order of significations in nature with the moral order by granting the power to read nature to a tried, tested, and purified hero-exegete, and to construct the novelistic action in such a way that it comes to a resolution as the hero attains the power of reading, and hence the power of truly understanding the world.

Nothing in this scheme sets Van den Heever apart from the run of nineteenth-century and early twentieth-century rural realists, except perhaps a heightened emphasis on the attainment of the power of reading, an emphasis which of course pushes to the forefront, sometimes clumsily, the problematics of signification and gives rise to accusations of "dualism" from critics in favour of a smoother, more naturalized, more disguised transition from the stage of "objectively realistic representation" ("realism") to the stage of interpreting the real—constituted now as an order of signs—a stage which they seem to regard as "romanticism," forgetting that interpreting the real has always been a part of "realism."

Was Van den Heever unable to achieve smoother, more deceptive, more "natural," less "dualistic" effects simply because he was a clumsy novelist? Yes; but this is only part of the answer. For at the centre of Van den Heever's art, at least in his *plaas-romans*, lies the epiphany, the moment of transition not only from the experience (or suffering) of reality to the interpretation of reality (attainment of the power to read signs truly), but from one form of consciousness (individual, death-directed) to another (lineal, life-directed). The orientation of the novels is thus not toward whatever message the illuminated consciousness is able to bring back from its explorations, but toward the representation of the illuminated consciousness itself, specifically as an ideal Afrikaner consciousness.

The kind of reading that sees Van den Heever as (I caricature the position somewhat) an escapist Romantic entangled in a medium in which he is not at home thus fails to see the goal of his enterprise: to unite a social philosophy of agrarian conservatism (a conservatism in reaction against both capitalism and socialism, one that finds its most sustained literary expression in the German *Bauernroman* of the years 1900–45) with an ingenious Romantic anti-individualism which advocates the submergence of the individual not in the race (as in the "blood-consciousness" preached by the later D. H. Lawrence) but in the family line.

5

Simple Language, Simple People:
Smith, Paton, Mikro

I

In her fiction, particularly in her dialogue, Pauline Smith writes a variety of English intended to sound simple, rustic, direct, and slightly archaic. To the reader who knows Afrikaans it carries clear echoes of that language. Seeing that she did not come from a family in which Afrikaans (or Dutch) was spoken, and left South Africa at the age of twelve, it seems reasonable to ask how much Afrikaans Smith did in fact know, how firm the foundation was on which she based her imitation.

In his monograph on Smith, Geoffrey Haresnape answers this question, supporting his answer with quotations from Smith's South African journal of 1913–14: she understood the language only imperfectly and could not speak it. Haresnape prints extracts from a letter she wrote, half in joke, in Afrikaans, as evidence that her grammar was faulty and her vocabulary elementary. Discussing the stylistic features of her prose, he argues that a subtler but more important influence upon her than spoken Afrikaans was the English of the Authorized Version. He quotes from the late essay, "Why and How I Became an Author," where Smith attests that the rural Afrikaans she remembered from her Little Karoo childhood "fell . . . naturally in translation into the English of the Old Testament." Haresnape concludes that what she was calling to mind when she wrote her books was not simply Afrikaans but Afrikaans filtered through seventeenth-century English (124–27).

I see no reason to disagree with this conclusion. But it raises further questions. How could someone whose Afrikaans was so rudimentary produce one of the more convincing imitations in English of Afrikaans speech-patterns? And why was it that to Smith the rhythms of rural Afrikaaans and Old Testament (i.e., Authorized Version) English seemed to fall "naturally" together? Are the two languages objectively more alike than Afrikaans and late nineteenth-century English, or may there have been an extralinguistic motive at work that made Smith *want* to hear them fall together? Further (and here the question is of a more general nature), for the writer who thinks of herself as rendering the speech, thought, and experience of people of one culture (for example, rural Afrikaners) in the language of another (for example, in English), should the language she writes be a culturally neutral variety or should it be marked stylistically as different, foreign (as Smith's Afrikaans English is)? If the latter, ought the practice of marking not logically to hold as well for the translation of written texts, so that a German text comes out in a German-sounding English, and so forth?

As phrased here, the question seems a foolish one, treating as a matter of logic what has long been a matter of convention. But it is not always wise to dismiss foolish questions. South African fiction is full of examples of people (and peoples) to whom a language limited and simplified in various ways is attributed, and whose range of intellection and feeling is by implication correspondingly limited and simplified. I will therefore take the risk of treating the question seriously.

In run-of-the-mill fiction—to simplify matters, I will confine my discussion to English-language fiction—there are common conventions for dealing with the speech of people whose native language is not English. Sometimes they are given "broken English," a dialect rarely particularized to the extent that identifiable native speech-patterns emerge, though the odd native word may be dropped in a moment of stress *(Merde!, Caramba!, Donnerwetter!)*. More often the practice is to give them a simple, functional, but on the whole fluent, even idiomatic English, which is understood to be a smoothed-out rendering of some hypothetical original about which neither author nor reader need trouble himself. The rendering of the thought—as opposed to the speech—of such characters is not typed by language: the question of whether thought occurs within the patterns of the native language is by convention dismissed as academic.

These are only two of a number of conventions that may be called on. But as a generalization it is fair to say that a linguistically particularized rendering of the speech and thought of nonnatives is rare in fiction. A corollary is that when foreign speech is rendered in a particularized manner, this is usually done for well-defined reasons, mainly for simple comic effect. In the translation of genres in which there is only a single speaking voice, a positive effort is usually made to domesticate the foreign: a translator will thus try to make a German lyric sound like a lyric written in English, erasing rather than carrying over the marks of its linguistic origin.

Whether we look at Smith as a novelist working with foreign material or as a translator of Afrikaans culture, her enterprise— preserving (or sometimes in fact creating) marks of origin for her material—is therefore an unusual one. For this process I will reserve the name *transfer,* which I will define as the rendering of (imagined) foreign speech in an English stylistically marked to remind the reader of the (imagined) foreign original.

Since the elaboration of an appropriate set of stylistic markers (in Smith's case, mainly a set of particles and syntactic inversions) and the deployment of such a set over the face of the text (over those portions of the text where an Afrikaans consciousness is directly or indirectly being represented, plus certain authorial portions into which the practice is allowed to spill over) is no mean task—certainly more of a task than setting in train one of the better-established conventions for the rendering of the foreign—it is fair to ask what intention lies behind the practice and what the practice achieves. The answer I will suggest is that Smith is concerned to assert certain myths about the Afrikaner, or rather to back existing myths with what will look like evidence, namely, the trace of a characteristic Afrikaner consciousness inscribed in his language, or in his language as thrown into relief through the medium of transfer. In particular, Smith's practice of transfer is meant to validate the homegrown Calvinist myth in which the Afrikaner has his type in the Israelite, tender of flocks, seeker after a promised national homeland, member of an elect race *(volk)* set apart from the tribes of the idolatrous, living by simple and not-to-be-questioned commandments, afflicted by an inscrutable Godhead with trials whose purpose is to test his faith and his fitness for election.

If this myth of the Afrikaner about himself was received in Britain with amusement or condescension, it was received with considerable sympathy too, even after the South African War. With sympathy, I would suggest, for a number of reasons, all reflecting domestic British concerns: uncertainty about where industrial civilization was leading; unease about the decline of the rural way of life in Britain; and nostalgia for pastoral solutions to historical problems, nostalgia reinforced by the strong pastoral strain in English literary culture. As for the historical consequences of the Afrikaner's myth of election and of the indulgence with which it was received abroad, I will say no more than that they have been far-reaching and serious. The question I will limit myself to is: How does Smith's practice of transfer help to validate the myth?

The answer would appear to lie in a mixture of linguistic accident and artistic design. Seventeenth-century English is somewhat more receptive than present-day English to the reordering of sentence constituents in the interests of emphasis and cadence—for example, to the shifting of prepositional phrases and direct objects to the beginning of the sentence. Afrikaans too permits, and sometimes prefers, these constituents in sentence-initial position. So when attempts are made to imitate Afrikaans syntax in English, and when these attempts are backed by a conscious effort to maintain a vaguely old-fashioned diction and, at heightened moments, to fall into the rhetorical figure of parallelism, we have results like the following, in which the respective influences of Authorized Version prose and Afrikaans syntax can only with difficulty be disentangled. (In creating a hypothetical and somewhat overliteral Afrikaans original I have followed Smith's ordering of elements, which coincides with one of the natural Afrikaans orderings.)

> Every bit of news that came to her of Klaartje and Aalst Vlokman Jacoba treasured. Against neither of them could she harbour any bitterness, of neither of them could she think any evil. Only when word came to the valley that Klaartje had married young Herman du Toit was she troubled. [B 118][1]

> [Elke brokkie nuus was haar bereik het omtrent Klaartje en Aalst Vlokman het Jacoba weggebêre. Teen geeneen van hulle kon sy bitterheid koester, van geeneen van hulle kon sy kwaaddink nie. Slegs wanneer woord die vallei bereik het dat Klaartje met jong Herman du Toit getrou het was sy verontrus.]

Pauline Smith's command of Afrikaans in real-life situations was slight and almost wholly passive. But command of a language is not identical with knowledge of it. There is a range of patterns, structures, socially characteristic terms that Smith seems to know very well, or at least to exploit to the limit of her knowledge. For her own purposes, in composing her texts, she had available to her a body of linguistic knowledge more extensive than any she was able to command in conversation. Let me outline, on the basis of *The Little Karoo* and *The Beadle*, what her knowledge must have included.

Smith uses few Afrikaans words untranslated, and where she does her spellings betray that she had read little Dutch (*Hoeg Straat* for *Hoogstraat* [*LK* 27]; *ribitjes* for *ribbetjes* [*B* 200]). On the other hand, there are a number of terms that she takes over either by a process of literal, element-by-element translation or else via English cognates. Some of these were or have become accepted South Africanisms (*ride transport* [*LK* 23]; *teach school* [*LK* 45]; *lands* in the sense of *landerye* [*B* 247]), while some remain neologisms: *thankoffering* (from *dankoffer* [*LK* 20]), *June month* (*Juniemaand* [*LK* 48]), *sweat-leaf* (*sweetblaar* [*B* 170]), *heart-thief*

---

1. The abbreviations used are: *B* for *The Beadle; LK* for *The Little Karoo.*

(*hartedief* [*B* 201]). (That Smith was acquainted with *hartedief* as a term of affection and knew that *Juniemaand* rather than *Junie* is used to indicate iterativity, suggests that her passive Afrikaans lexicon was far from slight.)

I have come across only one instance where Smith invents an English word on an Afrikaans morphological model: "a well-doing [= prosperous] young man" (*B* 88), on the model of *welvarend* < *vaar goed*.

Afrikaans possesses a number of particles, among them *nou, dan, maar, nog, wel,* whose semantic properties are highly complex, and mastery over which constitutes one of the more formidable barriers for learners of the language. A common and facile stratagem for giving Afrikaans an English flavour is to translate these particles in an inflexible way or retain them in typically Afrikaans positions in the sentence. Here are some examples of the stratagem from Smith; all occur in dialogue.

1. "And who *then* [*dan*] is Aalst Vlokman?" (*B* 17).
2. "Drink *then* [*dan* (*nou*)], Aalst Vlokman" (*B* 71).
3. "You cannot *now* [*mos*] have two wives" (*B* 33).
4. "Take *now* [*maar*] Betje [as wife]" (*B* 108).
5. "Leave *now* [*nou*] the . . . paper" (*LK* 91).
6. "Move *but* [*maar*] a little, beadle" (*B* 86).
7. "See *first* [*eers*] if she sits in the garden" (*B* 87).

To each of these examples corresponds a hypothetical Afrikaans original. To each also corresponds an English translation (or several alternative English translations) of the hypothetical original that does not employ a particle on the Afrikaans model and renders the sense of the original more accurately within the overall system of the English of Smith's time and class, that is, that would have been a *truer* translation:

1a. "And who may Aalst Vlokman be?"
2a. "Come on, drink, Aalst Vlokman."
3a. "After all, you can't have two wives."
4a. "Settle for Betje [as wife]."
5a. "Come on, put down the paper."

6a. "Move over a bit, beadle."

7a. "Go and see if she is sitting in the garden."

The function of the transferred particle is thus no more than to mark the speech as un-English, as stemming from an Afrikaans original.

Related to the transfer of particles and, like this transfer, confined to dialogue, is the practice of literalism: translation word by word within the phrase, sometimes with the false cognate deliberately selected. Though the hypothetical Afrikaans original is grammatical within Afrikaans, the resulting English sounds like the English spoken by an Afrikaner with a poor command of the language:

8. "You must first *say for me* [*vir my sê*] . . ." (*B* 33).

9. ". . . *by* [*by*] my father's house" (*B* 51).

10. "Fetch *for the beadle* [*vir die koster*] some water" (*B* 71).

11. "She *also* [*ook*] is gone" (*B* 225).

12. *"What say you [wat sê jy]?"* (*B* 231).

From a strictly logical point of view, such literalisms are indefensible. But they are also revealing.

The following two points emerge from detailed examination of literalism in the transfer of verb forms.

A. English makes certain aspectual distinctions via the form of the verb which Afrikaans has to make by the use of modifiers. Afrikaners with an inadequate command of English frequently carry over into English the habit of making aspectual distinctions via modifiers, or else fail to make them, producing sentences which to English speakers sound odd or even bizarre. In examples 13 and 14 below the Afrikaans verb form in the hypothetical original *a* is grammatically acceptable, while the aspect that results in *b* from transfer into English is unacceptable:

13a. "Loop kyk eers of sy in die tuin sit. . . . Sy sit gereeld daar."

   b. "See first if she sits in the garden. . . . She sits often there" (*B* 87).

14a. "Slaap hy nie?—"Hy slaap nou."

   b. "Does he not sleep?"—"He sleeps now" (*B* 211).

These examples bring the logical fallacy of transfer into sharp focus. No one speaking his own language makes errors of aspect: the time-system of the verb is too fundamental to language, and therefore to conceptualization, for that to happen. (Errors must of course be distinguished from the use of social or regional dialects from which specific aspectual distinctions have disappeared.) The errors in the above examples—the use of habitual rather than continuous forms—cannot therefore be attributed to the hypothetical personages who, behind the "real" speakers of sentences 13b and 14b, speak the hypothetical Afrikaans originals 13a and 14a: they belong solely to the process of transfer.

B. When Andrina speaks English to her English lover, she has a tendency to use *did* plus the infinitive where a native speaker would use the preterite:

15. "I did look for it" (*B* 112).
16. "I did know a little. . . . I did try . . . to read" (*B* 56).

Recourse to *did* + infinitive is common among Afrikaners with an uncertain command of English: not only does it allow the speaker to bypass irregular verb inflections, but it follows closely the pattern of the regular past formation in Afrikaans: *het* + *ge-* + infinitive. But what is one to make of the following example? Mevrouw van der Merwe is reading a letter. The narrator reports *in propria persona:*

17. All this did Mevrouw read sitting quietly (*B* 243).

On the one hand this is like Andrina's *did* forms; on the other, it follows the rule in English, now archaic, that allows the direct object to be preposed in the sentence, followed by the auxiliary and the subject. This happens to be a not uncommon emphatic pattern in Afrikaans. Thus we encounter here an overlap between forms that are aberrant because archaic in English and forms created by the process of transfer from Afrikaans, an overlap exploited by Smith to persuade the reader, by stylistic means alone, that turn-of-the-century rural South Africa *is* the past.

There are cases, particularly in *The Little Karoo*, where transfer is used with a heavy hand to achieve comic effects:

18. "If I plant me now my lands surely by the time it comes for
    me to . . . gather me my mealies I shall be dead" (*LK* 56).
19. "Both you and your clothes after you will I send out of the
    Kombuis" (*LK* 79).

These are the two most extreme examples of (apparent) transfer
that I have come across in Smith. But if, using the guideline of
literalism, one tries to reconstruct the Afrikaans behind the English, one finds that neither pseudo-original sits easily in the
volksmond (popular speech). The truth seems to be that as soon as
Afrikaans syntax gets beyond a certain fairly elementary level of
complexity, Smith's grasp on it weakens and her ability to play
upon it becomes unsure. One says *Ek plant my lande* and *Ek koop
my 'n plaas*, but not *Ek plant my my lande;* one says *Ek stuur jou weg
en jou klere agterna*, but not *Jou en jou klere agterna sal ek wegstuur.*

The novelistic practice with which Smith was comfortable gave
the writer several conventions for reporting the thoughts of characters, including the conventions of reported speech ("She
thought: Does it matter?"), indirect speech ("She wondered
whether it mattered"), and free indirect speech or *style indirect libre*
("Did it matter?"). The key characteristic of free indirect speech is
that the presence of a narrating intelligence is not asserted: the
narrator slips behind or into the intelligence of the character.

The signals that a shift into free indirect speech is taking place,
established gradually during the second half of the nineteenth
century, are varied and often subtle. Even today only some of
the reading public can be relied on to pick them up. Pauline
Smith has the distinction (as far as I am aware) of adding one
device to this repertoire of signals. The ubiquitous pressure of
transfer occasionally (in *The Beadle* but not *The Little Karoo*) allows
her to use constituents that follow the model of Afrikaans as
markers for transitions from an (English) narrating intelligence
to a character's (Afrikaans) thoughts, rendered in a free indirect
mode. The following are examples of such transitional moments
(the first Afrikaans-based constituent is italicized in each case).

20. She dared not, indeed, put her thoughts into actual words.
    If the sacrifice of the life and death of Christ were so won-

derful and personal a sacrifice as the pastor said, it must be some fault in herself that made it *for her* so meaningless (Andrina, *B* 75).

21. There were moments indeed when it seems as if he [the Englishman] alone . . . were real. And what though the beadle did not like him? *Had* the Englishman *need* of the beadle's friendship? Did one need a lighted candle in a sunlit world? Like the sun itself was the love she had in her heart for the Englishman (Andrina, *B* 93).

Thus far I have discussed (with one or two exceptions) inversions of standard English word order as they occur within the limits of the phrase. There also occur, however, syntactic reorderings on a larger scale in which phrasal constituents are shifted out of their usual position to conform more closely to an Afrikaans pattern:

22. In all but her household duties had Andrina, up in the Caroline district at Mijnheer Cornelius's sheep-farm of Uitkijk, found herself in a world that was new and strange to her (*B* 256).

23. Every bit of news that came to her of Klaartje and Aalst Vlokman Jacoba treasured. Against neither of them could she harbour any bitterness, of neither of them could she think any evil (*B* 118).

The shifting of modifiers, complements, and logical objects, via clefting constructions, to positions ahead of the verb is a particular feature of passages like the following, in free indirect speech:

24. Like the sun itself was the love she had . . . for the Englishman. Though no one else in all the world should love him, still, like the sun, would her love light up his world (*B* 93).

25. Thirteen years it was since he had come back. . . . Thirteen years had he worked the lands (Jacoba, *B* 118).

In the rendering of the direct speech of characters, un-English inversions are as much the rule as the exception:

26. "Weak he was from the day he was born, and weak he was all the days of his life. . . . In the market-place I cried, '. . . Full

of grace and the glory of God is his mind. . . .' And I said then also: 'True it is that Ludovitje goes but seldom to school . . .' " (*LK* 113).

27. "If I marry Toontje, three sheep will she bring to my kraal, and if I marry Betje, there will be in our house the sewing-machine" (*B* 33).

Sentences like 22–25 remain acceptable to English speakers, though they would probably be considered archaic. But the last sentence of 26 and example 27 are likely to be branded as substandard. It is difficult to argue that the key differences between the acceptable and the unacceptable types here are purely syntactic, since the same kinds of inversion occur in both. It is rather the case that more latitude for inversion is granted when the diction is elevated or simple-but-noble—in other words, when the subject matter is "literary" enough—than when it is mundane. The beginning and end of 26 illustrate this opposition neatly.

It is a convenient accident for Smith that the same syntactic device, and a simple one at that, can connote so many things, and that the connotations can be controlled by raising or lowering the level of the diction. Inversion can indicate any of the following:

a. in dialogue (low diction): that the speaker is a (simple, rustic) Afrikaner who, depending on what he says, may be either
   i. a clumsy figure of fun, a yokel, or
   ii. a straight-speaking yeoman, nature's gentleman;
b. in the twilight zone between narrative and dialogue: that a shift is occurring from authorial presentation to the free indirect speech of a native Afrikaans speaker;
c. in narration: that the field of reference of the discourse (rural life, the Little Karoo, the Africa of the Afrikaner) is one to which an archaized form of representation is appropriate, that is, *natural*.

The mode of Pauline Smith's work is elegy, its overall tone nostalgic. It looks back to a lost world: in terms of Smith's life, to her childhood in the Oudtshoorn district; in terms of history, to rural South Africa before the internal combustion engine. The elegiac mode is common in South African literature, particularly among Afrikaans writers: it is the mode of the generation that left the land, under various economic pressures, to live in cities. What sets Pauline Smith apart from her Afrikaans coevals is contact with an indigenous language (the language of a native, a man of nature) close enough to her own English in some of its characteristic structures to be domesticated simply by the process of *faux-naif* translation that I have called transfer, and access to stylistic resources available only in a language with a long written history, which together enable her to create in the echo chamber of the English prose tradition felicitous effects that cohere neatly with the Afrikaner's myth of himself as Israelite.

II

In Alan Paton's *Cry, the Beloved Country* (1948), the Reverend Stephen Kumalo, whose son is charged with murdering a white man, is told that a prominent advocate will appear for the defence *pro deo*. How can he afford an advocate's fees, Kumalo asks. His friend replies:

— Did you not hear him say he would take the case pro deo? . . . It is Latin, and it means for God. So it will cost you nothing, or at least very little.
— He takes it for God?
— That it what it meant in the old days of faith, though it has lost much of that meaning. But it still means that the case is taken for nothing. [125]

Kumalo's friend is partly right, partly wrong. The words *pro deo* used to mean, and still mean, "for God." In a legal context, however, they mean "without payment." The information about God is interesting historical background, but it carries as little semantic weight as the information that *martial* once contained a reference to Mars. Words do not bear their histories with them as part of their meaning.

Elsewhere in Paton's novel, Kumalo—a country priest on his first visit to Johannesburg—has gold mining explained to him by a fellow-Zulu:

We go down and dig it [the ore] out, umfundisi [sir]. And when it is hard to dig, we go away, and the white men blow it out with the fire-sticks. Then . . . we load it on to the trucks, and it goes up in a cage, up a long chimney so long that I cannot say it for you. [16]

Just as the (English) speech of Pauline Smith's Afrikaans characters is marked for Afrikaans origin, the speech of Kumalo's informant here is marked for Zulu origin, not only by the transcription of Zulu words like *umfundisi* but by words like *fire-sticks* (i.e., dynamite), *chimney* (i.e., shaft), and *go away* (i.e., take cover), as well as by an ungrammatical use of the English definite article ("the fire-sticks"). The reader cannot be blamed for concluding that Zulu lacks words for the concepts *dynamite, shaft, take cover,* that the speaker is using the best approximations his language provides, and that Paton has given literal translations of these approximations, in accord with the practice of transfer.

In fact this conclusion is false. The Zulu for mine shaft is *umgodi,* a word quite distinct from *ushimula,* (chimney), whose English origin is clear. The word for dynamite, again of English origin, is *udalimede,* which has nothing to do with fire-sticks. *Banda* (to take cover) is clearly distinguished from *suka* (to go away).

Thus while Paton uses the same principle as Smith, his practice has a shakier linguistic foundation. Smith's Afrikaans transfers are based on a more or less accurate, if limited, knowledge of Afrikaans. Paton, on the other hand, is content to create the *impression* that a transfer from Zulu has taken place. We see the trick most clearly in the phrase "the fire-sticks." Zulu speakers speaking English often have difficulty with the English article, since Zulu has no corresponding lexical form. But it is of course a mistake to conclude that Zulu speakers cannot make the semantic distinctions for which English relies on the article. "The fire-sticks" merely reproduces a common mistake made by Zulus speaking English; it says nothing about Zulus speaking Zulu.

The overt purpose of transfer is to make the reader imagine the words he is reading have a foreign original behind them. The artificial literalism of passages like the above, however, conveys in addition a certain naiveté, even childishness, which reflects on the quality of mind of its speaker and of Zulu speakers in general.

One of the more poignant conversations in the novel takes place—in Zulu, we are told—between Kumalo and James Jarvis, the father of the man whom Kumalo's son has killed. The two meet by accident. Jarvis, who does not yet know of the tragic connection between them, speaks:

—You are in fear of me, but I do not know what it is. You need not be in fear of me.
—It is true, umnumzana [sir]. You do not know what it is.
—I do not know but I desire to know.
—I doubt if I could tell it, umnumzana.
—You must tell it, umfundisi. Is it heavy?
—It is very heavy, umnumzana. It is the heaviest thing in all my years. [180]

What motive can Paton have for writing *be in fear of* instead of *be afraid of*, *desire* instead of *would like*, *heavy* instead of *serious*? In each case the synonyms translate the same putative Zulu original. In each case the choice is stylistic. The first member of each pair has a touch of archaism; this archaism makes for a certain ceremoniousness in the verbal exchanges, whose effect it is to hold any unseemly display of emotion at bay (the sentimentality of *Cry, the Beloved Country* is largely a matter of ostentatious stoicism of this kind). But the archaism of the English implies something else too: an archaic quality to the Zulu behind it, as if the Zulu language, Zulu culture, the Zulu frame of mind, belonged to a bygone and heroic age.

The Zulu original implied by Paton's English is both unrelievedly simple—there is a minimum of syntactic embedding—and formal to the point of stateliness. In its closeness to its historical roots, in its preference for parable over abstraction (Paton explicitly compares it to the "symbolic language" of parable [108]), Zulu—Paton's Zulu—seems to belong to an earlier and more innocent era in human culture. From the fact that Kumalo's politician brother prefers to use English, the reader may further surmise that Zulu is as inhospitable to lies and deception as it is to complexity and abstraction.

The phantom Zulu of *Cry, the Beloved Country* is in fact less the medium through which Paton's characters speak than part of the interpretation Paton wishes us to make of them. It tells us that they belong in an old-fashioned context of direct (i.e., unmediated) personal relations based on respect, obedience, and fidelity. These values are epitomised in an episode towards the end of the book. Jarvis has begun to send a daily gift of milk to the children of Kumalo's village. The man who brings the milk tells Kumalo: "I have worked only a week there [at Jarvis's farm], but the day he says to me, die, I shall die" (238). Self-sacrificial loyalty of this kind won for the Zulus the admiration of Victorian England; it is clearly a virtue Paton approves of. But these words also give us to understand that, by his receptivity to "Zulu" speech and his "Zulu" qualities, Jarvis has crossed the barrier between white and black and taken the place of the chief in his servant's heart.

What, if anything, then, separates Paton from those writers of the 1930s and 1940s who, under one disguise or another, call for the movement of history to come to a halt, for economic, social, and personal relations in the South African countryside to freeze forever in feudal postures? The answer is that, with however much regret, Paton accepts that the economic, and hence the political, basis of feudalism has been eroded by demographic forces. Kumalo's aspiration, in the wake of his son's death, is to hold together the remnants of his community in a muted version of black pastoral. But for how long? The fact is that the exhausted soil can no longer support them. As the young agricultural expert tells him, "We can restore this valley for those who are here, but when the children grow up, there will again be too many" (268). To this young man Paton allots the last and most telling word. To his logic Kumalo and his patron Jarvis, with their fragile hope of preserving an Eden in the valley immune from the attractions of the great city, have no response.

III

Between 1934 and 1944 the Afrikaans novelist C. H. Kühn, under the pen name Mikro, published a trilogy of novels concerned with rural life in the Karoo region of the Cape. The central character of the trilogy is a shepherd who goes under the nickname (awarded him by his master) of Toiings (Tatters). We follow Toiings from early manhood on Baas Fanie's farm, through three marriages, through bouts of town life, through the anguish of seeing his eldest son fall into a life of crime, to a final return to the farm, an older, wiser, and sadder man.

Because the sole language of the world of Coloured serfs and white masters that Mikro draws on is Afrikaans, the most obvious means for representing Coloured people as having a distinct kind of consciousness—by marking the language they speak and think in as of alien origin, as Smith does with her Afrikaners or Paton with his Zulus—does not present itself. Nevertheless, employing a range of differences, contrasts, and oppositions within Afrikaans, Mikro is able to suggest that two different worldviews coexist on the farm. Certain of the differences he exploits are stylistic, others are sociolinguistic, part of Afrikaans usage—or, to be more precise, part of Afrikaans usage in the rural South Africa of Mikro's day. Let me describe two of the latter differences.

1. In Afrikaans it is customary for parent to address child by the familiar second person pronoun *jy* while child addresses parent in the third person, as *vader/pa* or *moeder/ma*. In Toiings' world, in addition, master addresses servant as *jy* while servant addresses master in the third person. Asymmetry of address, which usually marks disparity of status between interlocutors, is by no means a phenomenon confined to Afrikaans. But social disparity is more usually reflected in the opposition of familiar to formal second person: the opposition of second person to third person would appear to mark a social divide that is felt to be particularly wide (Brown and Gilman 266–67), or else—in an authoritarian, patriarchal culture—a disparity of status much like that between parent and child.

2. Indo-European languages often have lexical subcategories based on a distinction between human beings and animals. In English, animals have *paws* or *hoofs* while human beings have *feet*. In Afrikaans, animals *vreet* (eat) while human beings *eet*. Afrikaans clings to human/animal distinctions with some tenacity: animal terms are not used of human beings without insulting

intent. But besides this subcategorization, Afrikaans has a further one, falling into disuse, perhaps, in the late twentieth century, but very much alive in Mikro's day, that marks off whites from *anderskleuriges* (people of colour). For the concepts man/husband and woman/wife, Afrikaans uses *man* and *vrou* for whites, *jong* and *meid* for other people. For boy/son and girl/daughter it uses, for whites, *seun(tjie)* and *dogter(tjie)* (*-tjie/-jie/-kie* is a so-called diminutive suffix, whose semantic function is various and complex), but, for other people, *klong/klonkie* and *meid(jie)*. Again, nonwhite terms are not transferred without insult.

The most interesting term in this racial sublexicon is *volk* (people). In one range of usage, as in *Afrikanervolk, Zoeloe-volk*, it belongs to the discourse of ethnicity and mystical nationalism. In an entirely different range, however, *die volk* is widely used for rural Coloured people in general, or for a particular Coloured community, or even for a particular farmer's Coloured work force ("Baas Fanie se volk").

What is significant about these racially defined distinctions— which inevitably convey hierarchy as well as separateness—is not that Mikro's whites use them, or even that his Coloured people use them in their dealings with whites—power has a way of inducing compliance—as that his Coloured people use them among themselves, even in their inner discourse. Toiings not only *thinks* of himself as a *jong* and of the woman he loves as a *meid*, but expresses his desire in relation to her as that of *meidvat*, literally "*meid*-taking," a racially bound term for marriage standing in contrast to the neutral *trou*. This internalization of the inferior status prepared for him by the language he speaks—a language which, here more than anywhere else, declares itself to be the language of the other, the white and the master—is intimately linked to his own low self-esteem. Having squirmed to think of his master laughing at his ambition to *meidvat*, he proceeds (in *style indirect libre*):

> If he were a better man [*jong*] he could greet [Siena, the woman he loves] with a kiss. But he was nothing more than a rubbish Hottentot [*weggooihotnot*]. . . . He was a bad Hottentot [*hotnot*], and he did not know why Baas Fanie was good to him. They had given him the right name—Toiings. He was as bad

as a dishrag or an old scrap of cloth on an ash-heap. But his child would be better. [*Toiings* 13, 16, 28. *Hotnot* is a disparaging abbreviation of *Hottentot*.]

Fatherly, all-knowing Baas Fanie emerges here as the castrator of Toiings' ambitions to manhood. Relinquishing his true given name (as "Friday" in the Crusoe story relinquishes his), Toiings accepts the name his master gives—objectively a name of derision, however much masked with affection—and becomes his master's creature. In a self-mystifying turn characteristic of what Gerwel calls his "slave mentality" (367), Toiings goes on to explain to himself his master's motive for incorporating him into his *volk* as one of disinterested benevolence toward the worthless child of a worthless race (a race of *hotnots*).

Toiings is an unsettled, questing figure: what action there is in the trilogy is generated by his restlessness. His quest is to understand the goal of his life. His inner discourse is marked by bouts of self-interrogation during which sparks of rebellion sometimes flare up. For instance, even if he himself cannot have a proper name, why should his son not have one?

> Something rebelled inside him. . . . Why must his son [*klonkie*] be born at such a disadvantage? Toiingtjies [Little Tatters]! The little thing had not sinned, after all. If he were one day to feel ashamed of bearing such a label, then he, Toiings, would quit these parts entirely.
>
> But the cool of evening brought relief. One after another the stars caught alight. The jackals began to wail. Still Toiings felt alone in the great spaces. And then his true spirit again triumphed, and he felt so guilty that tears of sorrow wet his stubble beard. Who was he, after all, that they should not name him Toiings, or Little thing [*Kleinding*] that they should not call him Toiingtjies? When Baas Fanie told him of eternity he felt small, as he did now. Small, but utterly content. Well, he would be content too, whatever they named his son. [*Toiings* 28–29]

Here Toiings passes through two clear stages. In the first, he rebels at the thought that his son may have to reproduce his own existence. In the second, he is reconciled to his (and his son's) lot as his "true spirit," that is to say, the voice he owes to the master who adopted him, reasserts itself within him as a guilt-inducing superego. The question Toiings has asked about the historical fate of himself and his descendants is settled by the voice embodied in him but speaking his master's language. This voice in effect reformulates his question as a metaphysical question about the soul and eternity. Toiings accepts the reformulation and retreats into childish quietude.

Elsewhere in the trilogy another voice of authority, the author's, makes itself heard to explain that the true reason for Toiings' inability to settle down and embrace hereditary serfdom is that he has yet to find enduring married love (*Pelgrims* 126–27). This takeover of the task of explaining Toiings prepares the way for the trilogy to reach its conclusion in the attainment of illumination by Toiings. Having lived through the disgrace and death of his son Dawid, Toiings returns to the farm. Meeting Baas Fanie, he begins to sob.

> "We heard [of Dawid's death], Toiings" [says Baas Fanie], "and the mistress and I thought a great deal of you. One day you will understand."
> Bravely Toiings said, "I understand already, master. The Lord takes the best, otherwise he would have taken me. . . . Dawid is in heaven, master." [*Vreemdelinge* 147]

In this exchange Toiings shows that, as the last word of the trilogy confirms, he has become a patriarch, ready to take up a minor position among the figures of authority. To Baas Fanie is allotted the role of raising the unsettling question: Why should Dawid have run away from the farm, bringing grief to his good father? To Toiings falls the role of explaining (with a self-deprecating twist) that it is all part of an inscrutable design, that all earthly contradictions will be resolved in the next world.

While the Toiings trilogy gives every appearance of allowing its protagonist to explore his destiny, and indeed seems to present the reader with a means of access—*style indirect libre*—to the inner processes of his exploration, what happens in practice is that Toiings' quest is continually sidetracked, derailed, or falsified. The resources of language and intellect granted to him are not enough to prevent him from being fooled. The questions he is allowed to formulate for himself are not the questions that really concern him, while the answers he arrives at are not even his own, but emanate from voices of authority speaking through him.

What are the real questions that concern Toiings? They are the questions posed, not in his musings, but by his bodily actions, actions without which there would be no story. They are posed most obviously by his restless to-and-fro (which Baas Fanie thinks of as Hottentot wanderlust) between farm and *lokasie* (location, satellite township). For a capable, sober, hardworking man, ask Toiings' movements, what ambitions are realizable as a shepherd on a white man's farm and what ambitions in the *lokasie*? On the farm, his capital—his flock of sheep and goats—can grow, but there are no goods to exchange it for. Yet the price of security of tenure is a degree of unquestioning obedience to the prescribed way of life—a way of life involving frequent ritual self-abasement disguised as piety—that Dawid, for one, refuses to accept. In the *lokasie*, capital can be exchanged for women, for liquor, for the prestige that largesse brings, but it cannot be made to grow. For a man whose skills lie in sheep-handling but who is barred by the law from owning land, is there any avenue left open but to accept a state of feudal dependance on a patron/master like Baas Fanie and hope to live in modest prosperity? There is none, Toiings concludes. But the voice in which he articulates this conclusion, the voice that articulates the conclusion in him, goes further: Toiings not only embraces his lack of choice, says the voice, but loves it too: "Toiings felt so nicely at home in his hut [on the farm]. . . . It was as if this were the corner of the world where one day he would not mind dying" (*Toiings* 145).

The social order that Mikro advocates is a feudal order of mutual dependance and reciprocal obligations between masters and serfs, an order familiar to us from other *plaasromans* of the 1930s. The *plaasroman* grows out of the Afrikaner's anxiety that he will lose his economic independence and cultural identity if he leaves the land. Mikro's particular concern is to argue that the drift of Coloured serfs off the land will be no less destructive of the old order. What lent the Toiings trilogy urgency in its time, and what made of Toiings the archetypal "goeie hotnot" (good Hottentot) to a generation of readers, was that Mikro purported to show from the inside what temptations even the best of farm-servants faces—temptations, however, that a watchful, sympathetic class of masters, aided by the clergy, could help to overcome.

In 1942 Mikro published a further novel of farm life called *Huisies teen die heuwel* (*Houses on the Hillside*), in which, to the list of enemies of the old rural order identified in the Toiings trilogy—irreligion, lax morals, liquor, as well as the impersonal forces of economics and climate—he adds a new and subversive ideology. This ideology arrives on Baas Gert's wine-farm through the agency of a troublemaker named Moos, the jailbird son of respectable working parents. "Every time they let him out of jail he was a harder communist. . . . Back on the farm he lounged about and blew all kinds of ideas into the *volk*'s ears" (41).

Mikro can still afford, in 1942, to introduce—though with genial contempt—a "communist" on to the farm. But when it comes to allowing him his say, he loses his nerve. The conflict that threatens between Moos and Baas Gert is not allowed to come to a head. Moos is killed in a brawl, the critique of feudal relations he promises to articulate never finds its way into words, and by the end of the novel Baas Gert is able to conclude that the failings of his *volk*—mainly work-shyness—are the failings of children, to be corrected with a kindly but firm paternal hand. The killing off of Moos—a failure of craft as of nerve, since after his death the novel drifts into inconsequentiality—is thus only another example of the baffling and silencing of any countervoice to the voice of the father/farmer.

6

Blood, Taint, Flaw, Degeneration: The Novels of Sarah Gertrude Millin

There is therefore a poetics of blood. It is a poetics of tragedy and pain, for blood is never happy.

—Gaston Bachelard

I

The Nuremberg war crimes trials, and what they revealed to the world about the implementation of National Socialist race theories, put a stop to a certain way of talking about other human beings: as low-grade people, degenerate types, *Untermenschen*, the unfit, slave races, and so forth. These terms, with their claim to stand for biological and anthropological realities, disappeared from public discourse, taking in their train a number of phrases involving *blood* (*blood-consciousness, pure blood, tainted blood*, etc.), as well as certain terms from the fringes of the science of heredity (*taint, flaw, degeneration*).

We cannot be sure whether the repression that occurred after the Nuremberg revelations—a repression with many components, including a will to forget, a horror of repetition, and, in Germany, a purging of the language itself by the occupation authorities—means the end forever of the form of race-consciousness exalted by National Socialism, or whether, having gone underground for a while, it will reemerge in mutated form. But 1945 so clearly marked an epoch both in the history of the West and in the development of anthropology that it seems unlikely that racial science in the Nazi mould will ever again flourish.

A measure of the power of the repression that came after 1945 is given by the fact that in South Africa, where a party with Nazi sympathisers in high positions was elected to office in 1948 and set about a program of racial legislation whose precursor if not model was the legislation of Nazi Germany, political prudence dictated that the rationale for race classification, race separation and race dominance should not be couched in terms of eugenics and biological destiny. In fact the public language of the National Party in South Africa has undergone Byzantine elaboration since 1945 to keep from voicing the key opposition—*über* versus *unter*—that was uttered with such confidence by Nazism in its heyday.

What is striking about the discourse of racism before 1945 is its nakedness, its shamelessness. "The old predatory instinct [has] subserved civilization . . . by clearing the earth of inferior races of men," wrote Herbert Spencer in 1851 (21). "No woolly-haired nation has ever had an important 'history'," wrote Ernst Haeckel in 1873 (2:415). Missionaries "turn healthy, though primitive and inferior, human beings into a rotten brood of bastards," wrote Adolf Hitler in 1924 (367). "The Griqua type of half-caste . . . is lower than the Kaffir," wrote Sarah Gertrude Millin in 1926.[1] One no longer comes across judgments like these expressed in public, even in South Africa (as to whether they live on in the private realm, who is in a position to judge?). So remote does the biologized history seem that formed their basis, that we might conclude they are best left to oblivion.

Ideas like these, however, once claimed a basis in what passed for scientific research and for a long while were viable intellectual currency. They formed part of one of the dominant myths of

---

1. *The South Africans* 202, hereafter abbreviated *SA*. Abbreviations used for other books by Millin are: *AR* for *Adam's Rest; GSC* for *God's Step-Children; CL* for *The Coming of the Lord; HW* for *The Herr Witchdoctor; KB* for *King of the Bastards.*

history from the mid-nineteenth to the mid-twentieth century, the myth that Western Europeans were biologically destined to rule the world. In what follows I will sketch the lineage of one element of this myth, the complex of ideas, images, and fantasies that express themselves in notions of *blood, flaw, taint,* and *degeneration,* particularly as the complex occurs in the work of Sarah Gertrude Millin, a writer of considerable achievements, certainly the most substantial novelist writing in English in South Africa between Olive Schreiner and Nadine Gordimer, neglected nowadays because her treatment of race has come to seem dated and even morally offensive. Millin's ideas on race, I will suggest, are not a mere hotchpotch of colonial prejudices but an adaptation of respectable scientific and historical thought, only barely out of date at her time; further, her emphasis on race is at least in part a response to formal problems that faced her as a colonial writer working in the medium of the novel.

II

A key word in those novels by Millin that deal with South African society is *blood.* It is a key word because, to Millin, it is in the blood that the most fundamental distinction between peoples is marked. Blood distinguishes African from European, Englishman from Afrikaner, Hottentot from Xhosa, Gentile from Jew. Blood is thus race; but, unlike the abstraction of race, Millin's blood is also a fluid that can be thick or thin, hot or cold, healthy or diseased; a quintessence of blood flows from man to woman in sexual intercourse; the same blood courses through the living embryo as through its mother, bearing in it the microscopic determinants that decide whether the child shall have straight or curly hair, blue or brown eyes, a fair or a dark skin. It is the poetics of blood rather than the politics of race that sets off Millin's imagination.

Millin is by no means the first writer to meditate on, and be fired by, blood. When she wrote her first novel, *The Dark River* (1920), she was able to take from other sources a well-developed image-repertoire. Later on I will discuss some of her sources. For the present it is enough to observe that the thematics of blood had occupied both writers and scientists for decades before 1920, that Millin took over an established system as a vehicle for her fiction (though it also makes a degree of sense to say that the ideology of racism, through its myth of blood, took over Millin as a vehicle through which to utter itself), and that she returned to blood with a repetitive insistence that we can properly call obsessive.

Millin's principal novel of blood, and the novel for which she is still best remembered, is *God's Step-Children* (1924), a novel of middling length but of dynastic ambitions in the manner of Zola or Galsworthy. Like Zola, Millin is concerned to trace the history of a *flaw* through several generations of a family, in this case the flaw of *black blood*. By tracing the course of ideas of blood through her novel, we in turn can get a sense of the generative power they held for her.

In part I of the novel, an English missionary, Andrew Flood, arrives at an isolated mission station on the Orange River. Unprepared by temperament or training for the task that awaits him, he finds himself first ridiculed and then ignored by the Hottentots he hopes to convert. In the hope of winning their confidence he goes through a Christian ceremony of marriage with a Hottentot woman and fathers two children. His light-skinned daughter grows to womanhood, sleeps with a passing white stranger, and bears an even lighter-skinned son, Kleinhans.

In part II Kleinhans tries to pass for white but is exposed and spurned. He marries a "Coloured" woman from the Cape, who bears him a daughter, Elmira. In part III Elmira, under the patronage of Kleinhans's employer, is sent to a white convent school. But the secret of her parentage emerges, and she is asked to leave. Thereafter she consents to a distasteful marriage with her patron and bears him a son, Barry, to all appearances white, before running off with a stranger.

In part IV (each part of the novel marks a stage in the ascent of the family toward the heaven of whiteness), Barry is taken to Cape Town for his schooling by a spinster half-sister. He proceeds to Oxford, takes holy orders, and returns to South Africa with an English bride. Eaten up with jealousy, the half-sister reveals the secret of his ancestry to his wife. Though at first she cannot understand why there should be a fuss about it, the wife's peace of mind is gradually eroded by the colonial obsession with race, and she asks to be allowed to return to England before their first child is born.

At this point news reaches Barry that his mother is on her deathbed. He returns to Griqualand West, where he resumes contact with his poverty-stricken family. The realization grows in him that his true home is with "my brown people," and he resolves to spend the rest of his life working among them.

It is a mistake to ask whether Millin is for or against the attitudes toward genetic inheritance that make it impossible for Barry to live a normal life with his English wife in South Africa; or at least it is a procedural error to ask the question too soon. For it is Millin's desire to argue that there is no way in which Barry, being Barry, can be happy. "Those . . . who must always suffer, are the mixed breeds of South Africa," she wrote in a preface to a 1951 reissue of the novel (xii). Barry's suffering was predetermined a hundred years before when Andrew Flood coupled with a Hottentot woman. His doom has been passed on to him in his blood. The question of whether one is for or against his suffering, for or against the mere mechanism—ostracism—though which his suffering is realized, thus becomes, in Millin's argument, as secondary as the question of whether one is for or against the suffering of Oedipus. All one's human pity may flow out to the victim. Nevertheless, his suffering was fated.

Whatever her motive, Millin is writing in the mode of tragedy. She is writing a *tragedy of blood,* intending to evoke responses habitual to tragedy, specifically the religious emotion of awe at mystery. The first inquisition should therefore properly be of the genre she has chosen. What are the elements of her tragedy of blood, and how does she believe it possible to write tragedy in a postreligious age?

Characteristic of the flaw passed down the line of Andrew Flood's descendants is that, for two generations, as long as they do not deny their racial inheritance, it does not come into play. It emerges from dormancy in the third and fourth generations, the light-skinned Elmira and Barry. But its power threatens to be strongest in the generations to come, in Barry's unborn child and all its descendants. The flaw can thus be thought of as "black blood" insofar as this blood is invisible—that is, hides in "white blood"—but also insofar as it threatens to erupt in the future, throwing off its white disguise, thereby retrospectively revealing all the past white generations of its carriers as frauds, false whites.

The flaw is thus like an inherited reminder of a fall from grace, the grace of whiteness, into a state similar in many respects to a state of sin. This similarity enables Millin to use the language of religion almost interchangeably with the language of popular genetics, particularly in part IV of the book, in which much of the narrative is mediated through the consciousness of Barry and his half-sister, both of whom lead active religious lives. They think as follows: "All this evil Barry had in his blood to hand on further" (220); "His skin was as white as anybody's. 'But it isn't only the skin,' some inner voice would whisper" (227); "Who knew but that he, Barry, had made poor innocent Nora [his wife] the vehicle of the vengeance of the Lord for the sins of the fathers?" (284); "For my sin in begetting him, I am not to see my child" (306).

The evocation of supernatural sanctions in what Millin calls "the tragedy of mixed blood" (xi) may seem merely opportunistic on her part, given that the basis of her thesis that miscegenation brings unhappiness lies not in Calvinism or any outgrowth of Calvinism but in the semiscientific, seminovelistic notion of degeneration: though the line of Flood may seem to be getting whiter, a subtle degeneration is being passed on too, and may manifest itself at any moment. But until the concept of degeneration is explored in all its often tautological complexity, one is not in a position to pass judgment on Millin's brand of tragedy.

III

The practical successes of science and technology in nineteenth-century Europe, the growth of industry, colonial expansion, and the dynamism of commerce convinced the broad, educated public that the world was becoming a better and better place. To a minority within that public, on the other hand, the great European empires were coming to resemble nothing so much as the

Roman Empire in its latter years, sick unto death behind the exterior of might and opulence, their sickness betrayed by the squalor and degradation of their great cities, but also, more subtly, by the doubt and self-questioning that infected their more sensitive minds.

Science did not close its eyes to these evidences of malaise. Its response took the form of a broad movement to define and isolate degenerate elements in civilization: neurasthetes, morbid depressives, hysterics, epileptics, syphilitics, sexual inverts, people of criminal disposition, alcoholics, opium addicts. Even the decadent artist did not escape its watchful gaze.

In retrospect one can see that the entire medical and psychological science of degenerativity was an attempt to expel unsound members from the social body, and that despite its proclaimed stand of objectivity, its ends were powerfully ideological (was the stance of objectivity itself not perhaps a mask for an ideological intention?). Given the confidence of positivist science that material causes could be found for all phenomena, the movement was bound to take on the form it did; but, except insofar as its purpose was one of scapegoating, it was also bound to fail, for it sought a psychological and ultimately biological explanation for what was a cultural condition.

The response of Emile Zola to the science of degenerativity is an interesting one.[2] Zola is fascinated by the varied case histories the scientists examine, and indeed in his propaganda for an "experimental novel" claims to take over the case history method of Claude Bernard. In his Rougon-Macquart novels he builds on some of the more lurid of the case histories to emblematize the decadence of France of the Second Empire. However, Zola's overriding thesis is that degeneracy or decadence is not an affliction of individuals who can simply be removed from society (for example, by being imprisoned or institutionalized or sterilized): society itself is an organism, and the degeneracy of individuals is in fact a symptom of the sickness of the social body. The Rougon-Macquart are not only a tainted family, they are a disease in the blood of France that eventually brings about madness and death

2. On Zola's scientific reading, see Carter 71–79.

in France's rulers. The disease is carried to the aristocracy by Nana,

> a young girl born from four or five generations of drunkards, her blood tainted by a long inheritance of misery and drink, which was transformed in her into a neurotic derangement of her female sexuality [i.e., nymphomania]. . . . Large, beautiful, with superb flesh like a plant growing in pure dung, she revenged the beggars and derelicts whose issue she was. With her, the corruption that had been allowed to ferment in the people rose and corrupted the aristocracy. She became a force of nature, a ferment of destruction, without herself wishing it, polluting and disorganizing Paris between her silken thighs, curdling it as women monthly curdle milk. [*Nana* 2:1269]

The ambition of Zola in the Rougon-Macquart novels is thus to demonstrate how social injustice returns as a vengeance upon the guilty rulers. To carry out this ambition he employs a master figure of disease, corruption, and inherited degeneracy, elaborating and extending it by whatever means the science of his day offers.

The vocabulary of degeneracy ("bad blood," "taint," "flaw," etc.) was common to nineteenth-century medicine and naturalistic fiction and was still very much in the air in Millin's earlier years. The notion of degeneracy as a biological means whereby a legacy of evil may be passed on to succeeding generations was also so much part of the stock-in-trade of popular science, and fitted in so comfortably with Calvinist warnings of the visitation of the sins of the fathers upon the heads of the children, that it is not surprising that Millin came to adapt it to the perils of interracial intimacy in South Africa. Similarly, the notion that "the native" is in some sense a pure type, and the deviation from purity represented by the half-breed a degeneration, was part of the intellectual baggage of British colonialism: it was given a first "scientific" formulation by William Lawrence in 1822, but, as Nancy Stepan demonstrates, this merely rationalizes older anxieties about "improper" sexual unions (105–07). Degeneration was commonly appealed to in late nineteenth-century Britain to explain away various unsavoury effects of urbanization upon the poor (Nye 64–67). All in all, then, although Zola brings together numerous currents in the theory of degeneracy in an exemplary way, it is not necessary to argue that Millin absorbed Zola or followed his example. Rather, both Zola and Millin (Millin belatedly) write under the influence of the European science of degenerativity of their day.

IV

The set of interlocking biocultural theories that explain the rise and fall of groups within societies and the rise and fall of societies themselves is known as Social Darwinism, though in fact the theories were current before the publication of *The Origin of Species* in 1859 (Harris 122–29). Social Darwinism in essence teaches that groups fail to flourish because there is something "in" them that is teleologically unsound. These groups are (tautologically) labelled unfit. Thus Social Darwinism in its crudest form explains the poverty of the poor, the enslavement of the enslaved, the criminality of the criminal as in some sense biologically predetermined, and so provides a scientific basis for a totalizing ethic in which "incidental suffering" can be ignored as "the great scheme of perfect happiness" unrolls (Spencer 21).

With hindsight it is easy to see to what ideological needs Social Darwinism answered in the advanced countries of the West. At home it explained why the rich got rich; abroad it explained why certain peoples were destined to be colonized. "Competition, progress, perfection, expansion, struggle, conquest—these were the themes, dynamic and optimistic, which [by the mid-nineteenth century] awaited a joining with the biological interpretation of history," writes Marvin Harris. "The fusion of these diverse elements into one grand scientific theory was the achievement of Herbert Spencer and Charles Darwin" (105).

Thus it is not strange that anthropology, as it grew to be a respectable academic discipline—that is to say, as it became institutionalized—should have centred on the study of race. One of the great tasks it set itself was to produce a taxonomy of human races within an evolutionist framework, to decide which were superior and which inferior and thus to predict what future might be expected for each. Nor is it strange, on the other hand, that the biologized history created by anthropology, a history whose ideological function was after all to justify the triumph of the West to itself, should in certain quarters have gone hand in hand with a pessimistic, fin de siècle outlook. For with the key term *progress* undefined save tautologically as the survival of those fittest to survive, why should one not foresee and even look forward to the triumph of the barbarian, rather than the reign of universal light?[3] Even a movement within the Darwinian intellectual tradition like German National Socialism, which is not usually thought of as pessimistically oriented (it envisaged a thousand-year Reich, after all), sees the German state as threatened by its own degenerate elements and conceives of its perpetuation in terms of continual and violent regenerative purgings of the body by its barbarian (Teutonic) core.

Several of the strains I have described occur in Millin: a respect for the authority of science; a belief in heredity as the key to history; a division of men into powerful, unreflecting barbarian types who "make" history, and weak, intellectual, civilized types who do not; a conception of history as a struggle of all against all for survival and mastery; and a pessimistic vision of the ultimate triumph of the barbarian. It would be too much to say that she brings these strains together into a coherent overview of history. It is nearer the truth to say that these are some of the elements of her intellectual baggage, which she picks up and uses as she sees fit, usually under the dictation of more obscure needs, including not only her own need to justify the political policies she favours, but also the needs of the novel form itself, in particular its need for rich metaphoric systems and diverse typologies of character. Nineteenth-century science provided her with a metaphorics of blood and a typology of race.

V

The idea of the blood as the locus of life and identity is as old as our civilization. As life-fluid, blood can "run high" or "run

3. See, for example, Thèophile Gautier: "Rather barbarism than *ennui!*" (quoted in Steiner 18).

slowly," "rise" or "freeze," be "hot" or "warm" or "cold," "thin" or "sluggish." Every state that blood as a fluid can be imagined to assume, in fact, can be metaphorically correlated to a psycho-physical state of the being through whose veins it runs. Hence, perhaps, the preoccupation of Western medicine till the twenti-eth century with the condition of the patient's blood.[4]

But unlike his limbs and organs, the individual's blood is not his property alone. Blood defines the inherited social status of the individual by flowing supratemporally through him and all his blood-ascendants and descendants: the blood of kings or slaves long dead can run in his veins. In this perspective, the individual is simply a carrier of the life of the family or caste or race: the analogy with theories of the individual as a vehicle by means of which the gene perpetuates itself comes readily to mind.

Because man is born not from one but from two, however, blood cannot be passed pure and unchanged from one genera-tion to the next. At each node of the family tree, a mother's blood is added to the father's. When these two bloods come together, the resultant is not a mixture of father and mother (it is at this point that folk-genetics, faced with the evident and awe-some variability of that resultant, collapses into superstition): the offspring can be like father or like mother or can take on "good" or "bad" features of one or both or can appear not to take on a feature and yet later on bequeath that feature to its own off-spring. Whether the blood is thought of as itself the determinant of the characteristics of the child who inherits it, or as the envi-ronment of a yet more rarefied life-fluid (Harvey's primogenial moisture) or of generative animalcules (Darwin's gemmules), it remains a fluid obeying its own inscrutable laws.

Nineteenth-century race theories take up both these concep-tions of the blood—as the fluid of generation and as the home of the germs of generation—as material for fantasy. In Gobineau,

4. See Hall. The blood theory of heredity was widespread among biologists in the nineteenth century and died out only after 1900 as Mendelian genetics became better known. For a while, in Germany under the Nazis, "Semitic blood" was segregated from "Aryan blood" in hospitals (Barzun 179).

for example, blood is conceived of as a fluid like wine capable of being watered down:

> The word *degenerate*, when applied to a people, means . . . that the people has no longer the same intrinsic value as it had before, because it has no longer the same blood in its veins, continual adulterations having gradually affected the quality of that blood. . . . Great peoples, at the moment of their death, have only a very small and insignificant share of the blood of their founders. . . . The blood of the civilizing race is gradually drained away by being parcelled out among the peoples that are conquered or annexed. [59–60, 67]

To Gobineau, the bearer of a civilization whose racial basis has been adulterated has become "a pale ghost": the vital redness of the blood of the founders grows weaker and weaker, till only a colourless liquid runs in their descendants' veins.

We find a similar image in the Goncourt brothers:

> Anaemia is overtaking us. . . . There is degeneration in the human type. . . . Perhaps that was the sickness of the Roman Empire, where the faces of certain of the emperors, even in bronze, have features that seem to have run. . . . [Then] when a society was lost, psychologically exhausted, a barbarian invasion would occur and transfuse into it the youthful blood of Hercules [quoted in Swart 112–13]

Here the opposition is between the thin-blooded, overcivilized degenerate and the red-blooded barbarian, who thickens the blood and reawakens vitality. Thinness of the blood co-occurs with physical and psychological symptoms of degeneracy, though it is not clear whether thin blood causes the degeneracy or merely marks it.

In Gobineau there is also a mathematics of blood-proportions at work: when a member of the "original" or "pure" racial stock mates with a nonmember, their offspring are only half pure, and so forth. Thus after the passage of generations, though the total volume of original blood in the population may be as great as, and indeed in theory greater than, the total volume present in the original generation, it will have become diffused so widely that within any given individual it will be "weak."

The notion of a blood-pool that is concentrated when the race is pure and diffused when the race is impure, that is to say, the notion of the population as a living reservoir for a certain volume of race-blood, leads naturally to historical narratives in which blood-stocks flow out in migrating waves, then mingle with other racial pools or absorb smaller tributaries or remain isolated and pure; or in which barriers and bulwarks are built to stem an influx of foreign blood.

Though it may seem only a short step from an emphasis on the blood-pool itself to whatever it is that enters into and adulterates the pool, the psychic distance is vast. In fantasies of adulteration, exhaustion, and paling of the blood, that which flows into the blood is weak, without strength or virtue or colour—in effect, water or some equally neutral fluid. But the fantasy of an invading foreign agent is dominated by images of poisons, germs, and nameless taints. We confront, in fact, not the mathematics of ratios of inheritance but the animistic magic of defilement. Thus whereas soberly scientific representations of the perils of adulteration of the blood-stock can be given, invasions of the bloodstream are typically presented in the language of paranoia. In Artur Dinter's *Die Sunde wider das Blut* (1918), for example, Jewish blood becomes a poison that lives on in the veins of a woman who has had intercourse with a Jew and prevents her from ever bearing Aryan children again.[5]

It is of the nature of paranoid obsessions that they should evade stable representation, and therefore that the imagery in which they articulate themselves should be inchoate, shifting, slippery under interrogation. There is no point in trying to pin down the defiling agent as a poison or a virus or a serum or anything else: it is, in Paul Ricoeur's words, "a quasi-material something that infects as a sort of filth, that harms by invisible properties, and that nevertheless works in the manner of a force in the field of our undivided psychic and corporeal existence." Defilement is "quasi-physical . . ., quasi-moral": "[Its] ambiguity

5. Dinter's novel is discussed in Mosse (142) and in Baur, Fischer, and Lenz (488).

is not expressed conceptually but is experienced intentionally in the very quality of the half-physical, half-ethical fear that clings to the representation of the impure" (25–26, 35).

Though we are nominally dealing with a defilement of the blood, a genetic defilement, the phenomenon of defilement is so strongly sexualized that the line between blood and sexual fluids is easily blurred. Thus in a document like Hitler's *Mein Kampf,* in which sexual-obsessional themes are closely linked to preoccupations with race, we can follow trains of association that lead within the space of a few pages from antiurbanism *(Grossstadtfeindschaft)* (since cities, as hotbeds of sexual stimulation, corrupt the youth), to venereal disease (as a materialization of that corruption), to the segregation of prostitutes (as prophylaxis against disease), to the segregation of infected (and therefore infectious) elements of the population, to measures against Jews, freethinkers, and artists (230–35). The importance of the spread of syphilitic infection as a model for fantasies of defilement cannot be overestimated. Like impure blood, syphilis is passed on from the impure partner to the pure in the sexual embrace and reemerges in their offspring as a *taint.* Like the carrier of impure blood, the carrier of syphilis in many cases bears no distinguishing mark and sometimes does not even know he or she is a carrier. Syphilis can "lie dormant in the blood" for years before manifesting itself. What lies behind the fantasy of genetic poisoning in Dinter's novel is obviously venereal infection; in the textbook on heredity that was standard in Germany of the Nazi period, the authors take such pains to spell out the difference between sexual transmission and genetic transmission that one must assume that confusion between the two was widespread (see Baur, Fischer, and Lenz 477–90). A syphilitic taint is, in Ibsen's telling metaphor, a ghost from a previous generation come to haunt the present; it is also a retribution, or, as moralists never tire of repeating, a sin of the fathers visited upon the children.[6]

6. Osvald Alving's doctor quotes these words to him when he first diagnoses syphilis (*Ghosts* 74).

VI

In Millin's poetics of blood, taint, flaw, and degeneration there are two kinds of blood, black blood and white blood.[7] Black blood is stronger and thicker than white blood (*GSC* 122, 184); thus it is white blood that dilutes black, rather than, as in Gobineau, black that dilutes white (*GSC* 284). Black blood has an earthy quality (*GSC* 226). Lindsell, the Englishman in *God's Step-Children*, marries a woman with black blood to strengthen his own, which is "poor," "thin," "meagre" (*GSC* 118, 149, 185). His pale son finds his mother's milk too strong for him, for in the poetics of body fluids, blood, milk, and semen share a common life (*GSC* 194).

When black blood and white blood run together, they "blend" and "mingle" (*GSC* xii, 269), yet retain their inherent identities. Thus in the veins of the half-caste run "on one side, the blood of slaves; on the other side, the blood of the careless, the selfish, the stupid, the vicious" (*SA* 205). There is no chemical binding or compounding of the two bloods. The man of mixed blood has two identities—"on one side . . . on the other side"—not a new compound identity. But instead of allowing him to belong to both parentages, his two identities make it impossible for him to belong to either. He can deny neither blood: when he tries to settle for one, the other will make itself felt "like acid" flowing in his veins (*KB* 52).

All acts of shame are recorded in the blood. The blood is thus a pool of unconscious memory passed down through the generations, and speaking in its own good time. A child may be born ethereal, white; then, as it grows older, its stronger, earthier black blood may utter itself (*AR* 156). In time of danger the

---

7. Millin's ideas on blood and race, and the complex of feelings that underlies these ideas, change little between 1920 and 1950. In sections VI–X of this chapter I therefore quote from a range of her writings without regard to chronology and with minimal regard to context. I have not drawn upon *The Wizard Bird* (1962), even though it is replete with blood-sacrifice, interracial coupling, and mental degeneracy, for it is a work of the feeblest imaginative power, a mere transcription of the isolationist paranoia and racial prejudices of the right-wing South African press of the times.

irresolute, divided quality of mixed blood particularly manifests ifself (*GSC* 262). The blood can even speak out like an "inner voice" (*GSC* 227).

What the blood remembers—besides the behavioural traits of remote ancestors (*GSC* 229; *KB* 11)—is above all the "sin," "shame," "sorrow," "evil" of the moment when the original mixing of fluids took place (*GSC* 90, 251, 279; *HW* 47). The parents of the new line, the Adam and Eve, are all too likely to be, on the one hand, a "slave," on the other "careless . . . selfish . . . stupid . . . vicious" (*SA* 205); their progeny will carry knowledge of their guilt in their veins.[8] This inherited guilt is a redoubling of original sin, flaw (*GSC* 266) in addition to Fall. Like original sin, their flaw is inescapable; unlike other forms of sin, however, it is unassuageable by confession, since he to whom it is confessed will be driven by the instinct of racial integrity to despise the one who confesses (*HW* 141).

Deeper than guilt, in fact, black blood is a form of defilement, a "stain" (*GSC* 230), "evil, sickness, dirt" (*HW* 47), bearing an instinctive sexual shame with it (*HW* 141), a formless horror evading description, creeping over the boundaries of all names. The only way in which the polluted community can return to purity is by expelling the defiler. Expelled, he will find a home only among other exiles (in Griqualand West in *God's Step-Children*, in the northern Transvaal in *King of the Bastards*).

The community's edict of expulsion comes in the form of ostracism, physical assault (the assault on Kleinhans in part II of *God's Step-Children*), outlawing (the outlawing of Buys in *King of the Bastards*); the first chapter of *King of the Bastards*, set in 1948, foretells that the edict is to be codified in the form of D. F. Malan's race laws. The edict is necessary because black blood has a will and a life of its own: it will "go further," spreading its defilement over the whole of the white community as a vengeance for the repressed evil of the past (*GSC* 71, 220). For it is the nature of taint that, no matter how thinly spread it is in the

8. In D. H. Lawrence's *The Plumed Serpent*, the spirit of the "moment of coition" between Spanish man and Indian woman is similarly "abject" and their progeny therefore abject-spirited too (68–69).

blood-pool of the community, it will remain itself, in this respect being not like a dye but like an oil.

To the white community, the return of outcast black blood looks like a vengeance upon it. The bearer of mixed blood, however, is driven not by thoughts of vengeance but by a (doomed) desire to eliminate his black blood by drowning it in more and more white blood (*KB* 2, 11). Only the exceptional man, like Barry Lindsell, realizes that what must be done is to kill the taint by sexual abstinence, by extinguishing the line that carries it (*GSC* 306).

VII

Blood Tragedy

Once black blood has entered the line, "there can be no more white children" (*GSC* 274). Children will be born "with shame and sorrow in their blood" (*GSC* 251). Begetting such children is a sin (*GSC* 306), one that opens the way for "the vengeance of the Lord for the sins of the fathers" (*GSC* 284). The vengeance of the Lord may take many forms: the birth of a throwback to a darker ancestor, for example, or the crippling of the individual by a contempt for his ancestry that is "one of the nails in the cross that the black-blooded bear" (*GSC* 226–7). No matter how white the guilty one's line may grow, his ancestral secret will not be safe: the "vagaries of heredity" (*GSC* 284) may at any time proclaim his shame to the world.

The flaw in the blood of the half-caste is thus an instinct for death and chaos. It destroys the peace of the community by revisiting its repressed sins upon it, it drives the half-caste himself to a withdrawal from life. Mixed blood is a harbinger of doom.[9]

---

9. It is clearly a productive irony for Millin that the biological fertility of the hybrid (which she explicitly points to in *The South Africans* 206) is the essence of his destructive power. Gilles Deleuze suggests that in Zola "flaw" is simply another name for the death instinct (44–49).

VIII

Race Purity

In *King of the Bastards,* Coenraad Buys goes through a ceremony of blood-brotherhood with an African chief which entails stripping naked and crawling through the belly of a freshly slaughtered cow. For days after the ceremony Buys feels unclean: "He had felt ridiculous, crawling after the fat black man through the body of the cow; standing there, before the yelling savages, so big, so white, so old, with the cow's mess all over his skin and upon his ears and eyes and mouth and nostrils and white hair and white beard and white man's pride" (267). The "mess" of the bloody rebirth shames him. Outlawed by the white community, he nevertheless cannot become the brother of his black ally in any but a nominal sense.

Those who deny having "colour consciousness," Millin pronounces, "are, biologically speaking, sports," or else deceive themselves. Colour consciousness is a "profound feeling (call it instinct or call it acquired prejudice)" and can be overcome only by another biological force, such as sexual desire (*SA* 255–56). Thus Buys can sleep with black women and father children of mixed blood but cannot give up his sense of having a racial identity.

The black man too has his "pure" racial identity. "Whatever else the black man might be, he [is] at least pure," say the whites (*GSC* 227). When a black woman marries a white man she is "raped of her black purity" and cannot regain it, even by subsequent marriage to a black man (*KB* 158).

The purer a black people, the more "aristocratic" it is. The Zulus are the most aristocratic of South African peoples, the Batlapi less so because more "mixed" (*CL* 110; *KB* 223). Hottentots, with their "Mongolian" faces, are at the opposite extreme (*GSC* 16). Pure black nations "once had a greatness of their own, and will have it again" (*GSC* xii).

Certain people argue that class divisions are more basic than race divisions (for example, Saul Nathan in *The Coming of the Lord*

99). Such people may, in a sense, be right. However, it is characteristic of them that they are ineffectual, asexual, thin-blooded. Therefore their views do not prevail in practice over those of the "full-blooded, active type of man" (*CL* 233), who wins the love of beautiful women, fathers strong children, makes history. The clash of ideas is subordinate to a Darwinian struggle at the level of the blood between the men who hold the ideas, and of the two the stronger-blooded will win.

IX

Blood-Mixing and Degeneration

When Andrew Flood arrives among the Hottentots, he is revolted by the "dirty, evil-smelling, vermin-infested reed huts" in which they live (*GSC* 13). But Hottentots are not uniquely smelly and dirty: "Kaffirs" too have a peculiar smell, the consequence of "dirt and neglect" (*GSC* 99). Kaffir women, in particular, have a "formidable acrid smell" (*KB* 62). Even missionaries who have lived among Africans for years do not grow used to their smell (KB 182), one that "taints the pure night air" (*KB* 211).

The smell of the black man marks him, at the most animal of levels, as a foreign species. But his smell is not merely foreign: it threatens the contagion of the dirt in the midst of which he lives and which he carries on and in him. What is this dirt? It is not only the dust and sweat that he does not wash off, the fats with which he anoints himself, the faeces and urine which he disposes of too casually. It is not only the flies that buzz around him and the germs that breed in his saliva. It is all of these and something more, something nameless, experienced, as Ricoeur suggests, as both moral contagion and physical defilement. Sometimes the thrust of this defilement reveals itself brutally. "Nine-tenths of the natives [have] syphilis" (*HW* 10). But it is its nature always to evade and exceed definition. Barry Lindsell tries to treat the threat as simply the threat of syphilis, "yet he could not help feeling the spirits of the natives too were sick with some frightful infection. He nervously washed his hands after taking theirs; but even his soul, having touched the sores of their souls, seemed to him in need of cleansing. He feared the contagion of the godless" (*HW* 10–11). Yet no more than it can be contained in the diagnosis of syphilis can it be labelled godlessness or barbarism. It is a dirtiness that goes beyond and beneath all language.

The force that drives white men to defile themselves with black women is never represented in Millin. The idea of the union of black and white is "thrilling" because "illicit," she suggests (*GSC* 123, 174), but that is as far as the curtains are opened. To gauge the force of transgressive desire we have no recourse but to measure the force with which it is repressed, that is, the force of the distaste with which the white man in a state of desire for the black woman is represented. Here is the missionary Van der Kemp:

> His head was now naked from his thick arched eyebrows to the sprouting white hairs to nearly the nape of his neck. On the other hand, hairs, white and black, grew out of his nostrils and ears; and a bristle of white hairs covered most of his face. . . . Coenraad looked from the bald old white man with the sprouting white hairs to the little dark frightened girl standing beside him [his bride]. [*KB* 184, 186]

When he speaks of his black women, Van der Kemp's face wears "an ecstasy" which Buys "had before noticed in senile men smitten with their sex" and which disgusts him (*KB* 178). Senile degeneration has in fact set in; hair, sprouting everywhere save where it should, betrays an animal sexuality no longer under the control of the decayed mind and longing to prey upon young flesh. Similarly, the "fleshless" old Lindsell marries his half-caste ward in order "to draw at the fountains of her youth, rejuvenation" (*GSC* 149, 145).

Apart from these two old vampires and the mentally degenerate Andrew Flood, white miscegenators are characterized only as "lonely, drunken. . . , careless and casual" (*GSC* ix, xii), "the careless, the selfish, the stupid, the vicious" (*SA* 205). Thus although Millin is prepared to involve tragic emotions in her "tragedy of mixed blood" (*GSC* xi), it is not the tragically incomprehensible attraction of the noble toward the base (as in Alan Paton's *Too Late the Phalarope*) that constitutes the flaw out of which disaster develops: Millin's is a naturalistic tragedy of victims subject to a biologized fate initiated by the meanest of lusts.

The fruit of such unions is that "unnatural creature" the hybrid (*GSC* 275), from whom pure-blooded women flee so that they "need not see those brown creatures, and think how they came into the world" (*GSC* 279). For though everyone is conceived sexually, brown people are in addition conceived in an act of sexual defilement. Therefore not only must they be objects of shame and outcasts, but they must inevitably be riven with hatred of their own being. Kleinhans hates the half-caste community in which he lives "for the blood that was in them" (*GSC* 84), and Carl Lindsell hates his own "black blood" as a "dirty sickness" (*HW* 47).

The hybrid is further damned in that the two bloods in his veins are debased bloods to begin with. The Adam of his line is likely to have been feeble of mind or ridden by senile lust, the Eve a woman from a "broken tribe" with no race pride left (*GSC* ix). His roots therefore lie in degeneracy passed down in the blood. Degeneracy is the Lamarckian mechanism by which history enters the blood and becomes heritable. Slaves and tribes that have lost social cohesion in the aftermath of conquest pass on the germs of slavehood and feebleness to their offspring (*GSC* xii, 293). Similarly, "poor whites" who have cut loose from familial ties degenerate, and as part of that process couple with black women (*AR* 42). Finally, alcoholism, malnutrition, and venereal disease leave their various taints in the blood (*AR* 67; *GSC* ix). The man of mixed blood thus remembers through his blood all the miserable history of his line as it degenerates from its original purity.

X

The representation of personal appearance by the novelist is never disinterested. It is an act of composition masquerading as an act of reading: pretending to read face, body, and dress as a constellation of signs, the novelist is in fact engaged in composing a figure out of them. What distinguishes Millin is her eye for ethnicity as she reads appearances:

> Little, yellow, monkey-like people, with . . . triangular faces (Mongolian . . .), and peppercorned heads. [*GSC* 8]

> Their fuzzy brown hair stood away from their heads in golliwog fashion. . . . They had yellow skins and brown eyes [*GSC* 47]

> She had the straight, coarse black hair and shadowed black eyes of the Cape girl. . . . She had the thin little nose, the well-cut mouth and the oval cheekline of her Malay grandmother, her German blood showed in her [pale] skin, and her voice too was light and gentle. [*GSC* 107]

> Barry . . . had soft, brownish hair. [*GSC* 107]

> Maria had a trace of Malay in her Hottentot face: the face was a little rounder, the eyes a little rounder, than if she had been a pure Hottentot, the nose was a little higher and the mouth and cheek-bones were not so high. [*KB* 27]

> Tetyana's . . . hair was brushed until his natural peppercorns were straightened into a massed woolly smoothness. [*CL* 110]

Features are being scrutinized here not for class indicators or for ruling passions or for aesthetic qualities, but for ethnic markings: from the features the racial ancestry is being read.

"For racial description and classification," writes Eugen Fischer,

> the most important characters are: the colour of the eyes and of the hair; the colour of the skin; the Mongolian spot [at the base of the spine]; the growth of the hair; the shape of the nose; the folds of the eyelids; the shape of the lips and other physiognomical details; serological distinctions; stature; the shape of the cranium; the shape of the face. [Baur, Fischer, and Lenz 165]

The best starting point for racial classification, writes Ernst Haeckel, is the hair, for "it seems to be strictly transmitted within the race" (2:414); and Haeckel goes on to create a taxonomy of race based on the microscopic analysis of hair.

Millin sticks remarkably close to Fischer's criteria, with heavy emphasis on hair texture, when she is dealing with Africans and people of mixed blood: more particularly in the latter case because there the body betrays its history of secret shame. But even when the milieu is wholly white, her cognitive set has a strong ethnic bias, seeking to pick out German or Jewish or Dutch or Anglo-Saxon features.

This schema of Millin's is the embodiment in novelistic practice of what we can justifiably call a racial consciousness. One can imagine what Millin's response to this charge might be: that in a "multi-ethnic society" like South Africa's, different ethnic types continually thrust themselves before the eye. The question is, however, whether the eye is ever innocent, whether it ever sees the world other than through its own cognitive paradigms. Would the whole scene of secret shame that Barry Lindsell's wife sees in the streets of Cape Town not vanish like a mirage if her desire to see it evaporated? Millin nowhere entertains this possibility, I would surmise because she remains locked in the ambivalence of obsessional sexual curiosity and sexual disgust. Failing to recognize the obsessional nature of her attitude toward what she calls the act of blood-mingling, she is debarred from recognizing the role of projection in the traces of ancestral sin she sees everywhere.[10]

It is not my purpose to speculate about the real-life origins of Millin's obsessions with race-mingling. However, there are strong reasons for questioning the account that Martin Rubin advances in his biography of Millin. Rubin writes that in her attitude toward miscegenation, Millin "seems to have taken over the prevailing attitudes wholeheartedly." He finds it "extraordinary" that "an intelligent and otherwise sensitive woman" should have held such attitudes. "The explanation may partly lie in her total lack of scientific, sociological or anthropological training. Had she been better informed on these subjects, she could not so easily have subscribed to such grossly unsupported notions." But the "deeper reason" was that she could not resist "the intense pressure toward racial prejudice" that came from her childhood environment (20, 82).

Few novelists have any training in science, sociology, or anthropology; this was even truer of Millin's generation than it is today.

10. The obsessional nature of Millin's recording of ethnic characteristics has been noted before: see Wade 104.

Nevertheless, Millin's novels reveal a clear acquaintance with the anthropological and social orthodoxy of the early years of the century, when the influence of Darwin and Spencer was predominant. Other writings of hers confirm this acquaintance.[11] What Rubin does not recognize is that, between Millin's formative years and the present, a radical change has taken place in anthropology, centring on the question of race. The stages of change can be followed in Marvin Harris's *The Rise of Anthropological Theory*. Millin is a child not only of the "isolation and intellectual sterility" of South African society (Rubin 82) but of the ethnocentrism of the sciences of man of her day.

XI

It is beyond my scope here to trace Millin's evolution from cautious liberal in the 1920s to supporter of Verwoerd in the 1960s. However, since I have hitherto concentrated on racist elements in her thought, I ought to emphasize two points at which the racist set of her mind is complicated by ambivalence.

1. Barry Lindsell recognizes that his son, unable to live in South Africa because of the "flaw" in his blood, will nevertheless be able to live happily in England. Thus Millin does not deny the role of the social environment of the individual in giving him a "white" or "black" identity.

2. Millin expresses repugnance for the thesis she encounters in Darwin that in the course of evolution "lower" races are exterminated by "high" races (*SA* 234), in spite of the fact that in *God's Step-Children* and *The Herr Witchdoctor* she depicts the remnants of "broken tribes" in the last stages of evolutionary extinction (*GSC* viii).

I mention these two points because the contradictions they raise are striking. In a fuller analysis one would be able to identify

11. In *The South Africans* Millin refers directly to Darwin's *The Descent of Man*. In a letter of 1966 quoted by Rubin (257) she mentions having read Darwin, Galton, and Julian Huxley. It is unlikely that she did this reading in her old age. *The Wizard Bird* has an anthropologist as a leading character and reveals a fair acquaintance with what fieldwork (at least the fieldwork of an anthropologist of a few decades earlier) entails.

many more points, I suspect, at which Millin's thought becomes, if not confused, then at least inconsistent. Confusion arises when her sympathies flow against the deterministic scheme in whose terms she has chosen to see human evolution. This conflict of sympathy with system occurs often, generating most of what we can loosely call the tragic interest of her novels. Insofar as the conflict is to Millin's advantage as a writer, a generator of writing, there is little incentive for her to remove its cause by carrying intellectual analysis further (to a point, for example, where the contradictions noted above might be resolved); and the more Millin baulks at further analysis, the less reason there is for taking her social or political thought seriously.

Millin's thought does, however, have historical importance to the extent that she reflected or indeed helped to create a climate of opinion in her time. One aspect of this historical importance has particularly concerned me here: I have linked her with the Nazis and have suggested that it was their fate to be discredited together. But the question immediately arises: how can one assert this link when Millin was a Jew, a fervent anti-Nazi, a friend of Smuts, and the author of a novel (*The Herr Witchdoctor*) that warned against the penetration of South Africa by Nazi propaganda?

The answer must be that, from our vantage point in time, the differences between Millin's anthropology and Nazi anthropology seem less important than the similarities. "National Socialism is applied biology," said Hans Schemm, cabinet minister in Bavaria; and in 1939 Ernst Rudin, director of the Kaiser Wilhelm Institute for Genealogy and Demography, wrote, "Our whole cultural life for decades has been more or less under the influence of biological thinking."[12] Millin's fiction, too, lies heavily under the influence of biological thinking, and at times becomes a form of applied biology. More important, her fiction is

12. Weinrich 34, 33. For an account of how, in the early years of this century, biological doctrine was bound into the nexus of antiliberal, anti-Enlightenment, anti-industrial, anti-Christian, anti-Semitic ideas that he calls "the Germanic ideology," see Mosse 88–107; also Cecil 67–69. To gauge the amount of anthropological research into race within this same biological tradition in the English-speaking world, see Dover's bibliography (293–306).

under the influence of the same variety of biological thinking as was Germany of the Nazi period. Millin refused permission for her work to appear in German translation, but *God's Step-Children* was pirated and read widely in Germany as a *Rassenroman* (Rubin 174). Although Millin was outraged, the fact must be faced that the Nazi sensibility found her horror of blood-mingling congenial.

XII

I have thus far treated Millin's interest in blood and race as something independent of her vocation as a novelist. While it is very likely that as a complex of emotional attitudes it antedates her first writing, there are nevertheless reasons why this particular obsession should have proved a fertile one for her.

Among Millin's problems as a novelist were two faced by every colonial novelist of her generation: the problem of deciding which elements of the European novel were relevant to the colonial situation; and the problem of locating in the colony a social field rich enough to support the transplanted European novel. These two problems are closely intertwined. Because the texture of colonial society is typically thin, rather than dense, and does not permit the play of social nuance on which the novel of manners is built, the colonial novelist has to look beyond the field of purely social interaction. The Romantic novel, with its emphasis on solitary destinies, provides an attractive model: Emily Brontë rather than Jane Austen. As American novelists of the first and second generations discovered, however, it is not easy to make novels out of the careers of people outside society. R. W. B. Lewis states the problem succinctly: "What kind of change is possible for the solitary figure surrounded by space?" (86). American fiction from Fenimore Cooper to Mark Twain is a succession of responses to this question.

Millin does not have the talent for an equivalently inventive response. Taking over the mainstream English novel of class, she simply extends its operations to a mixed field of race, class, and caste. To put this in another way, she decides to see conflict in South Africa in terms of race, class, and caste rather than in terms of class alone. She also takes over from Naturalism the apparatus of middlebrow physiology and psychology that allowed it to redefine destiny in terms comprehensible to a secular age and thus to continue to exploit the themes and emotions of tragedy.

A typology of characters on an ethnic rather than on a class basis is an inviting solution for a novelist seeking a system of characterological oppositions out of which to generate writing. Such a solution ought in theory to entail a radical rethinking of the novel as a form. The solution that emerges in colonial practice tends to be a mixed one: an ethnic typology for those parts of the novel set in the wilderness, a class typology for those parts set in society. This is the solution Cooper arrives at in his Leatherstocking novels (where society is represented in microcosm by the recurrent band of white adventurers), and this too is Millin's solution in novels as superficially different as *God's Step-Children* and *The Fiddler*. The utter failure of a novel like *King of the Bastards* can be explained as the result of too much of the "solitary figure surrounded by space," too much reliance on an ethnic typology of tribe after tribe that Millin has to elaborate out of her own entrails as she writes.

Any view of Millin as a woman imbued with the racial prejudices of white South African society and using her novels as a means of propagating and justifying these prejudices must therefore be tempered by a view of her as a practising novelist adapting whatever models and theories lie to hand to make writing possible.

7

Reading the South African Landscape

Europe and Africa

Among the poems Thomas Pringle wrote during his residence in South Africa in the 1820s is the prospect poem "Evening Rambles." For his British readers he describes some of the sights of the Eastern Cape, where

> The aloe rears her crimson crest,
> Like stately queen for gala drest;
> And the bright-blossomed bean-tree shakes
> Its coral tufts above the brakes.[1]

1. Sources for poems cited hereafter are as follows: Guy Butler, "Myths," "Servant Girl," "Cradock Mountains," "Sweet-water," "Farmer," "Home Thoughts," "Near Hout Bay": Butler 29–31, 33, 36–39, 40–45, 65–67, 72–76, 100–01; Roy Campbell, "Rounding the Cape": Campbell 124; Jan Celliers, "Die vlakte": Opperman 34–36; Sydney Clouts, "After the Poem," "Residuum," "Within," "Table Mountain": Clouts 75, 78–79, 80, 128–30; A. S. Cripps, "To the Veld": Butler & Mann 46; Patrick Cullinan, "1818. M. Francois le Vaillant Recalls": Butler & Mann 193–96; Anthony Delius, "Flying Home": Delius 7–8; H. I. E. Dhlomo, "Long have I worshipped thee": Dhlomo 354–55; H. H. Dugmore, "A Reminiscence of 1820": Dugmore 24–26; Charles Eglington, "Old Prospector": Eglington 30; Kingsley Fairbridge, "Africanders": Fairbridge 17; Uys Krige,

Though the flora may be strange to Britons, the poetic context in which Pringle sets them is not: the familiar trot of iambic-tetrameter couplets reassuringly domesticates the foreign content. The underlying argument of the poem from beginning to end is that, since the African wilderness clearly does not strain the capacities of the English language or even of English verse, it can be contained within the European category of the exotic. We can see the same programme of containing the exotic being carried out decades later in the execrable blank verse of H. H. Dugmore:

> Kareiga winds its devious course along
> Between its willow's banks; while here and there
> The dark leav'd yellow wood lifts its proud head
> In stately dignity.

> ["A Reminiscence of 1820"]

What we encounter in Pringle and Dugmore is the first and most cautious stage in a self-defeating process of naming Africa by defining it as non-Europe—self-defeating because in each particular in which Africa is identified to be non-European, it remains Europe, not Africa, that is named. The process is continued well into the twentieth century: here is Francis Carey Slater on the Karoo:

> Region bereft of the laughter of grass and its joy-giving
>   greenness,
> Barren of still woods dreaming Narcissus-like over their
>   shade:
> Alien to you is the music that gladdened Eve in her Eden—
> Harping of minstrel-rivers, fluting of light-footed rills.

> ["The Karroo"]

"Plaashek": Opperman 209; C. J. Langenhoven, "Die stem van Suid-Afrika": Opperman 95; C. Louis Leipoldt, "Die soutpan," " 'n Handvol gruis": Leipoldt 31, 193; N. P. van Wyk Louw, "Dennebosse," "Vier gebede by jaargetye in die Boland": Louw 3, 88–91; William Plomer, "A Transvaal Morning": Plomer 30; Thomas Pringle, "Evening Rambles": *Poems* 20–26; Francis Carey Slater, "The Herdboy's Flute," "In the Highlands," "The Karroo": Slater 18, 111, 210–13; Totius, "Trekkerswee": Opperman 49; C. M. van den Heever, "Aand op die plaas," "Hier op die skurwe randjierug," "Herfs in Holland": *Versamelde gedigte* 24, 60, 89; David Wright, "Flying to Africa, December 1969": Wright 20–21.

From here the directions that will be taken by the poetry of topographic description are almost predictable: either a more and more frenzied application of European metaphor to Africa in an effort to make it yield its essence; or the abandonment of defeated European categories in favour of a putative naturally expressive African language. We see Slater taking the first route in "The Karroo":

> At noontide the sun chastises the plain in his anger,
> Heat-rays flicker aloft, like chaff from a winnowing-floor;
> Glittering heat-waves leap, like spray that is tossed by the
>   surges,
> Leaping they shiver and sparkle silently flooding the plains.

Similarly A. S. Cripps, in "To the Veld":

> Ragged brown carpet, vast and bare,
> Seamed with grey rocks, scathed black with flame!
> Stage-carpet, foil to all that's fair.

A self-enclosed poetic dynamic is set up by these metaphoric excesses. Because they fail to compel the veld to yield up its essence, they are predictably followed by a reaction in which the veld is condemned as unresponsive to language ("What can you yield of delight to those who . . . / Seek for elusive Beauty, crave for the spell of her voice?"—Slater, "The Karroo"). One short step further, we can foresee, and the veld will become inscrutable and indifferent.

The other route involves, first, deciding that the real Africa will always slip through the net woven by European categories (Patrick Cullinan's "1818. M. le Vaillant Recalls" spells this out), and then wondering whether native African languages may not be in harmony with the landscape as European languages are not. Thus Guy Butler hears a Fingo woman sing a song

>   more integral
> With rain-rinsed sky and sandstone hill
> Than any cadence wrung
> From my taut tongue.

["Servant Girl"]

Slater's "The Herdboy's Flute" is a more complex (though not fully thought out) presentation of the same thesis: the Zulu herdboy who cannot answer the poet's questions about what inspires his flute music is both too stupid (too uninquiring, too unverbal) to comprehend that the leap from landscape to art (in this case the art of music) is in essence metaphoric, and too deeply embedded in his landscape (too unreflective, too unconscious) to need to know that landscape and art-response are not one and the same thing.

The debate has by now clearly led us to the point of uttering the central question occupying South African landscape poetry: How are we to read the landscape we find ourselves in?

The Language of the Veld

If literary landscape is not to be a secondary and inferior art, a mere verbal transcription of a scene already visually composed, it must do, or at least offer to do, something that pictorial landscape cannot: read out and articulate the meaning of the landscape. In its simplest form the reading process will simply put into words the mood that the landscape (or an imagined pictorial representation of the landscape) evokes. There is plenty of such mood-rendering in South African poetry, particularly in Afrikaans. Typically the mood of the landscape creates a mood in the poet, and the corresponding movement of the poem is from exterior to interior, sometimes proceeding so far that exterior and interior invert themselves and exterior becomes metaphor for interior (C. M. van den Heever time and again illustrates this movement; but the pattern holds for much of what seems at first sight to be landscape poetry in C. Louis Leipoldt and N. P. van Wyk Louw).[2]

There is a strain of landscape poetry, particularly strong in South Africa, however, which grows out of the venerable figure

2. "Herfs in Holland," rendering autumnal scenes in Holland, not South Africa, is Van den Heever's most orthodox landscape poem. Landscape description in Van Wyk Louw is surprisingly perfunctory, even in "Vier gebede by jaargetye in die Boland." Of the collected poems, only the early "Dennebosse" can be read as a landscape poem in its intention.

of nature as God's book (St. Bernard: *natura est codex Dei;* Coleridge: "The Universe in the most literal sense is [God's] written language" [339]), and which therefore foregrounds the problem of the meaning of the landscape and claims for poetry above other arts the craft of descrying meanings in the landscape. The questions that trouble white South African poets above all are, as we might expect, whether the land speaks a universal language, whether the African landscape can be articulated in a European language, whether the European can be at home in Africa. The most ominous answer is warned of in one of Leipoldt's poems: "Hier praat die veld 'n onverstaanb're taal" (Here the veld speaks an incomprehensible language) ("Die soutpan" [The Salt Pan]).

Charles Eglington, in a poem called "Old Prospector," presents an emblematic reader of the land in the person of a prospector who eschews the "eagle's view," the all-encompassing overview of Africa, in favour of a close poring over the earth. His "diviner's eyes" "read in cryptic signs / The formula for rich discoveries," for they understand "the veld's / Arcana." In effect he turns away from the comprehensive prospect-view of an older, colonial pictorial art linked to conquest and domination, in favour of a humbler homegrown art of closely rendered particulars, grounded on love of and intimacy with the land-as-soil.

This poem of Eglington's is noteworthy not only for the claim it stakes for a new landscape art not founded on the imperial gaze, but for reenunciating a recurrent theme of South African landscape writing: that the true South African landscape is of rock, not of foliage; and therefore that the South African artist must employ a geological, not a botanical, gaze. The originator of the idea is Olive Schreiner, in the early phase of her career when she was under the influence of her reading of natural history and evolutionary theory: the stones of Schreiner's Karoo speak to those trained to read them, though what they mainly speak of is the insignificance of man (Schreiner 49). This geological turn to South African landscape poetry is particularly intriguing because of its claim that vegetation *disguises* landscape, that traditional landscape art, the art of the prospect, is superficial by nature, cannot tell the true story of the land, the story that lies buried, or half-buried, beneath the surface. The new landscape art, calling on old analogies between distance and superficiality, closeness and depth, thus becomes above all an art of deep reading; the painter skilled in the representation of superficies is set aside in favour of the poet with his penetrative divining art.

What lies buried beneath the unpromising surface of Africa, besides lifeless metals? In Butler's "Sweet-water" it is water. Apprehended not by the eye but by the more primitive tongue ("Taste how sweet it is"), drunk in a reverential kneeling posture, the life-giving underground water of Africa offers itself to Africa's true children: the native, the primitive, the lonely diviner. In other poems, the stony truth of Africa emerges in the form of a flower: the africander violet that springs from the "beetling krantz" and derives its sustenance from the "fierce old mountain's heart" (Kingsley Fairbridge), the aloe that grows out of the "skurwe randjierug" (rocky ridge) (C. M. van den Heever, "Hier op die skurwe randjierug"). The rocky interior thus has a living heart, revealed only to the closely attentive observer, the lone walker of the wilds. The locus classicus of this epiphany in the veld is the moment in *The Story of an African Farm* when a tree utters its truth, or is on the point of uttering its truth, to Waldo (262).

The most remarkable of the geological landscape poems are those in which the poet's penetrating gaze reveals, not the superficial aesthetic form of the land, but an underlying prehistoric form threatening to erupt back into history. The earliest of these poems is Roy Campbell's "Rounding the Cape" (1927), in which, under the poet's seeing eye, the menacing contours of a sleeping black figure emerge from the mountains. In the Transvaal William Plomer sees "Shoulders of quartz [protruding] from the hill / Like sculpture half unearthed." Flying over the ancient dry seabed of the plateau, Anthony Delius wonders whether "Behemoth" does not lie "dreaming like a barbel under mud" beneath the dead landscape.

Side by side with these crypto-prophetic poems of giants and monsters on the point of waking out of an earthbound sleep of centuries to claim their due can be set certain more historically upbeat Afrikaans poems in which the landscape is figured, not without straining the reader's imagination, as a stretched-out

woman, even a mother (though a demanding rather than a boun-
tiful mother): Jan Celliers, "Die vlakte"; C. J. Langenhoven, "Die
stem van Suid-Afrika."

Guy Butler

The theme of the poet in the South African landscape has occupied Guy Butler throughout a long career. The poet in Butler is a
various and complex figure: the bearer of the creative imagination; the bearer of a European culture in Africa; man afflicted
with self-consciousness. The one familiar avatar we do not find in
Butler is the poet as a being who projects moods on to the landscape or is flooded by the mood of the landscape. That is to say,
Butler treats the relation of the poet to his landscape historically.

In moments of alienation recurring again and again, Butler's
memory throws up—and his poems relive—"spots of time" that
force on him an unsettling realization of his alienness in Africa,
perhaps in the world. For instance, in "Myths" he kills a cobra (in
this context one of the autochthonous creatures of Africa), and at
once the landscape ceases to be a comfortable environment: aloes,
boulders, lichens, clouds erupt into separateness, "all insisting on
being seen." This moment of alienation in which the world establishes its distance from the subject is also the moment at which the
landscape announces its resistance to language. Specifically, in
Butler's formulation, it is the moment at which African landscape
announces its resistance to European language.

> I have not found myself on Europe's maps . . .
> I must go back with my five simple slaves
> To soil still savage, in a sense still pure:
> My loveless, shallow land of artless shapes
> Where no ghosts glamorize the recent graves
> And every thing in Space and Time just is:
> What similes can flash across those gaps
> Undramatized by sharp antithesis?
>
>   ["Home Thoughts"]

Butler thus defines the difficulty of finding a language for
Africa as twofold: (1) the African landscape just is, without the

"depth" that landscape possesses when, from long association with a particular language, with the inherited and written culture of the people who speak that language, it comes to carry the historical resonances of voices from the past; while (2) (and here is the point at which Butler is notably acute) the route taken by poets from Pringle onwards who have described Africa as not-Europe, dramatizing it by antithesis, makes Africa into a mere negative reflection or shadow of Europe, insubstantial.

Throughout his later writing, Butler circles around the problems articulated in "Home Thoughts." Where he comes closest to falling into a response of rather easy Romantic primitivism is in poems that look wistfully to Africans or rural whites of an older generation as sharers in a lost but longed-for "natural" relation with the land. This primitivism is a feature of "Servant Girl" and "Sweet-water," already mentioned. It is most clearly thematized in "Farmer." Here an old Karoo farmer stares out over a landscape he has known all his life, a landscape that is "water and breath of life to him." The relation between this farmer and his landscape, the authoritative voice in the poem asserts, is "real": in inarticulate country folk like this one, whatever their moral failings, exists an unalienated feeling for the land that is killed off when the ascent into language is made. The corollary is that the very impulse to describe the beloved landscape is evidence of a fallen or alienated state; attempts to return to grace through art are foredoomed.

The most fully developed position taken by Butler on the question of a language for Africa is in the late poem "Near Hout Bay." Though this poem appears to deal not with the alienness of the landscape the eye beholds but with the alienness of the sounds of nature (cicadas, doves, wind, surf), one may assume there has been a mere transposition from sight to sound, and the crisis being faced is the same one. The point the poem makes is a familiar stoic one: that faith in the power of language to heal the breach between man and nature (as well as between man and man) has never been well founded, and it would be as well to "accept separation," as the ear accepts the "ignorant sounds" of the wilds without fretting about their meaning:

ten thousand sun-struck cicadas ecstatically screaming;
near and far hundreds of doves in relays
imperturbably repeating themselves to each other;
pine woods sighing into the wind from a thousand
    shimmering needles;
wind already burdened with the grumbling,
perpetual, unpitied
crumbling of the surf.

But, as a poetic speech-act, the poem itself paradoxically con-
tradicts its overt thesis, or attempts to do so: the lines quoted are
a rendering, a representation of the sound-scape near Hout Bay,
and (it emerges) an interpretation too: these sounds "fill that
primitive silence / with sadness and with praise." Butler's position here—that the various orders of nature, separate one from
another, nevertheless praise their creator as best they can, and
perhaps cannot help doing so—is thus significantly removed
from the conclusion that the enterprise of trying to read the
sights and sounds of Africa is misdirected. Indeed, it is not far
from *natura codex Dei*.

However titled, the poems by Butler thus far mentioned have
been about a generalized South African landscape. The poem
most closely tied to a particular landscape is "Cradock Mountains." This is also the poem that most clearly reveals the depth of
Butler's debt to Wordsworth: Wordsworth's reflections on the
power of remembered childhood scenes to "impregnate and ele-
vate the mind" and the bird-snaring and Grasmere Fair sequences
(*Prelude* [1805] 1.586–640, 1.315–332, 13.1–61) almost entirely
define its range and concerns. The poem raises a Wordsworthian
question—In what ways have I been moulded by the landscape in
which I have lived?—but barely begins to answer it. In being
content, as here, to play out themes from the English tradition
against an African backdrop, Butler settles for no less provincial a
goal than the Thomas Pringle of *Poems Illustrative of South Africa*.

Sydney Clouts

In Clouts, as in Butler, the relation of poet to landscape is at the
forefront of concern. But in Clouts the poet is a rather different

figure from what he is in Butler. He is neither a European nor the bearer of an alien European culture. Nor does self-consciousness or the possession of language seem to set him apart from his landscape. If he is set apart at all, it is only because his language has not yet attained the acuteness of penetration that will convey him into the landscape to become part of it, as he carries on his search for an interior Africa, an Africa in the interior of the Africa we seem to see. Language and consciousness are therefore not a burden to him. On the contrary, through the medium of the poet but also in the person of the poet the landscape achieves its fullest expression and fullest being.

> I am not contemplative by
> nature but *in* nature . . .
> Contemplative in nature means
> nature in me, my nature.

["Table Mountain"]

Entry into nature does not, however, come easily. It is achieved after a hard struggle with the resistance of the world, a struggle in which the principal organ of penetration and takeover is the eye. A poem called "After the Poem" expresses the will of the landscape to reassert its separate identity after the rape of being named, described, possessed:

> After the poem the coastline took
> its place with a forward look
> toughly disputing the right of the poem to possess it . . .
> The coast flashed up—flashed, say, like objections
> up to the rocky summit of the Sentinel
> that sloped into the sea
> such force in it that every line was broken.

But one should not be blind to the fact that, as a poem, "After the Poem" attempts to master and take over the landscape's very reassertion of itself. Poetry in Clouts is above all imperial.

The organ of mastery in Clouts (as in Wordsworth, who calls vision "the most despotic of our senses"—*Prelude* [1805] 11.174) is the eye. When the eye fails, "will not go in" (as in "Within"), poetry falters. But the goal of Clouts's poems is less to hold the landscape in the grip of sight (the goal too of landscape art, a form brought into being by the self-definition of the subject as the one who *views* nature, holds the scene in his gaze) than to enter the landscape via the eye in order to live its existence from inside it. For this purpose the overview that conceives the landscape as a totality, even a geological totality, has to be abandoned. The poems move instead with great rapidity from item to item of the landscape, taking over the life of each and then quitting it. The poet's eye is thus a devouring, voracious eye. For its part, the thing possessed begins to mutate and shed its old name almost as soon as it is taken over by language. The most remarkable of all Clouts's poems, "Residuum," is a kind of flickering of poetic force from object to object, the poem refusing to settle, since as soon as it settled it would be absorbed into the object. The life of the poem is thus, as it were, in the spaces between the lines:

> No lexicon, just one word accommodates us, quickly said.
> No word is my dwelling place . . .
> Listen, listen among the particles.
> A vigil of the land as it appears.
> Open, open.
> Enter the quick grain: everything is first . . .
> I am the method of the speck and fleck.

Clouts provides the most radical response as yet to the burden assumed by the South African poet of European culture: the burden of finding a home in Africa for a consciousness formed in and by a language whose history lies on another continent. To the charge that the poet show what position must be taken in order to see Africa as it really is—in other words, that he define a prospect position from which Africa will settle into a landscape "at home" in the categories provided by his language—Clouts responds by taking no position, or by taking all possible positions, thus denying the primacy the prospect position itself (the position of the observer) and proposing instead an unsettled habitation *in* the landscape.

National Landscape

Landscape poetry in South Africa has been written predomi-
nantly by people to whom English has been a *home language* and
the English literary tradition, however ambivalently regarded,
the tradition in which they have been *at home*. Among black
writers, even those of dual African-English linguistic culture, the
mode, without precedent in the vernaculars, has barely been
practised.[3] The thinness of landscape poetry in Afrikaans may,
however, seem surprising. For is the Afrikaner's claim to a national future in Africa not expressed (when not expressed in the
blunt terms of the pragmatics of power) in terms of a unique
relationship to the South African landscape, to which he claims
to be *native;* and would we not expect this claim, and the overriding love of the land asserted along with it, to find expression in a
well-developed art of landscape poetry? Yet the fact is that descriptive landscape poetry is rare in Afrikaans, and reflections
on the problematics of landscape writing even rarer.

Explanations for this state of affairs are not hard to come by.
Landscape art is by and large a traveller's art intended for the
consumption of vicarious travellers; it is closely connected with
the imperial eye—the eye that by seeing names and dominates—
and the imperial calling. The preconditions for such an art of
landscape writing have never been met in the history of the
Afrikaner. Not only that: the heyday of landscape writing was
over by the time Afrikaans emerged as a literary language.

Furthermore, the English-language poetry of landscape comes
out of a complex and philosophically developed poetics and aes-
thetics of landscape, whose great figures are Wordsworth and
Constable. Afrikaans has no corresponding tradition, and, where
it does work out of an alternative poetics (the poetics of Tachtig in
the Netherlands, for instance), is concerned (like Tachtig) not
with the problematics of representation but with the metaphysics
of sympathy between subject and landscape.

---

3. There are a few passages of landscape description in H. I. E. Dhlomo's
poems of the 1940s, mainly pastiches of the neoclassical pastoral: "Yonder the
herd-boys sing their sylvan songs; / And, cropping grass, crawl mute the motley
herds" ("Long have I worshipped thee").

An added explanation that might be advanced is that the concentration one encounters in English-language poetry on the alienness of a European language to an African landscape reflects a fact about English (and the stance of the English-language poet) which does not hold for Afrikaans: Afrikaans is as native (*inheems*) to Africa as any African language, it might be argued, and therefore fits over the African landscape "naturally."

The fact remains, however, that poems like Leipoldt's " 'n Handvol gruis," in which a handful of pebbles from the scene of childhood (in this case the region of the Hantam) evokes a world of memories and causes a sublime expansion of being, are rare in Afrikaans. The impulse that in less agrarian societies emerges in writing about nature seems to emerge in Afrikaans as writing about the childhood farm. The farm, rather than nature, however regionally defined, is conceived as the sacral place where the soul can expand in freedom. Thus in Uys Krige's poem "Plaashek" we find the wanderer returning to the farm where he was born and experiencing in the act of opening the farm gate the same intimation of a return to the true self and primitive moral sources that Wordsworth feels in returning to the dales and fells. The variety of freedom associated in Afrikaans literature with the farm harks back, certainly, to memories of carefree childhood, but also, in the course of historical time, and particularly from the 1920s onwards, to a lost ideal economic independence, to the idea of the farm as a "koninkrykie" (little kingdom), where a man can be his own master (Totius, "Trekkerswee"), and, by extension, to the enduring dream of a separate state, a "Free State" where the Afrikaner will at last be left in peace to run his affairs in his own way. The question should therefore at least be posed of whether the thinness of landscape poetry in Afrikaans may not reflect an indifference to nature by comparison with farm (nature parcelled and possessed) or land, as that richly polysemous word occurs in the Republic's national anthem: "Ons land Suid-Afrika" (Our land South Africa).

On the other hand, it should be borne in mind that the very notion of a "nature" somehow transcending the subjection of the land to laws of ownership belongs to a social class no longer relying directly on agriculture for its livelihood, and therefore to a more economically differentiated society than existed on any scale among Afrikaners till the 1920s. If one looks for absences in Afrikaans poetry, it is the absence of a John Clare—a poet from what can loosely be called the peasantry—that is remarkable, rather than the absence of a Wordsworth.

One should not overlook, furthermore, a mode of natural, or at least rural, descriptive writing in Afrikaans that has no parallel in South African English literature: a deft, quick, highly metonymic itemization of particulars whose effect is to evoke the mood *(stemming)* of the scene:

> 'n kafferstem klink hard ver oor die werf, . . .
> 'n stofwolk goud-omlyn rys bo die kraal,
> patryse skreeu daar ver; 'n sweepsklap dwaal
> deur die verlate lug in egos aan.
>> [C. M. van den Heever, "Aand op die plaas"]

> [from far across the farmyard comes a kaffir voice . . .
> a cloud of dust, outlined in gold, rises above the kraal,
> faroff partridges call; the crack of a whip
> lingers in echoes in the forsaken air]
>> [Evening on the Farm]

The high degree of particularity of this kind of evocation—as common in prose as in verse—is an index of a greater community of experience between writer and public than the English-language writer in South Africa has ever been able to rely on. It might even be argued that the sketch, the quick notation of telling particulars, as above, rather than full-scale, paragraph-long exposition, is the appropriate descriptive form for a society with considerable uniformity of background.

We have seen how the project of landscape-writing in English comes to be dominated by a concern to make the landscape speak, to give a voice to the landscape, to interpret it. This is not the ambition with which the landscape of Southern Africa was initially approached: writing in the twilight of neoclassicism, Pringle still regarded it as an appropriate field of aesthetic contemplation. But toward the middle decades of the twentieth century the confrontation between poet and landscape becomes more and more antagonistic, the poet wrestling with the silence of a landscape that "absorbs imagination / Reflecting nothing" (Wright) or struggling to interpret its cryptic signs. The desert of the Southern African plateau becomes the home of a Sphinx, a Sphinx all the more baffling for having no material form, for being everywhere present yet nowhere apprehensible. The Sphinx does not speak; yet, indifferent, more than indifferent because not even personally present to be indifferent, it forces upon the poet the role of a man answering a riddle, a riddle which he must, faute de mieux, lacking any interlocutor, pose to and for himself. The Sphinx he confronts is in fact no different from nothing; it is an absence, for which flat, windy, "empty" space under an even cloudless sky is at least as good a figure as the giants, giantesses, or monsters sometimes detected in the earth by an alert eye. Certainly there is the option of meeting the silence of the Sphinx with silence. But what is felt with the greatest urgency by these poets is that silence, the silence of Africa, cannot be allowed to prevail: space presents itself, it must be filled.

In all the poetry commemorating meetings with the silence and emptiness of Africa—it must finally be said—it is hard not to read a certain historical will to see as silent and empty a land that has been, if not full of human figures, not empty of them either; that is arid and infertile, perhaps, but not inhospitable to human life, and certainly not uninhabited. From William Burchell to Laurens van der Post, imperial writing has seen as the truest native of South Africa the Bushman, whose romance has lain precisely in his belonging to a vanishing race. Official historiography long told a tale of how until the nineteenth century of the Christian era the interior of what we now call South Africa was unpeopled. The poetry of empty space may one day be accused of furthering the same fiction.

Works Cited

Alexander, James Edward. *An Expedition of Discovery into the Interior of Africa.* 2 vols. London, 1838.

Anthony, P. D. *The Ideology of Work.* London: Tavistock, 1977.

Bachelard, Gaston. *On Poetric Imagination and Reverie.* Edited by Colette Gaudin. Indianapolis: Bobbs-Merrill, 1971.

Barrell, John. *The Idea of Landscape and the Sense of Place, 1730–1840.* Cambridge: Cambridge Univ. Press, 1972.

Barrow, John. *Travels into the Interior of Southern Africa.* 2 vols. 2d ed. London, 1806.

Barzun, Jacques. *Race: A Study in Superstition.* Rev. ed. New York: Harper & Row, 1965.

Bataille, Georges. *Death and Sensuality.* New York: Arno, 1977.

Baur, Erwin, Eugen Fischer, and Fritz Lenz. *Human Heredity.* 3d ed. Translated by Eden and Cedar Paul. London: Allen & Unwin, 1931.

Bergmann, Klaus. *Agrarromantik und Grossstadtfeindschaft.* Meisenheim a.G.: Anton Hein, 1970.

Beukes, Gerhard J., and Felix V. Lategan. *Skrywers en rigtings.* 4th ed. Pretoria: Van Schaik, 1961.

Blum, Jerome. *The End of the Old Order in Rural Europe.* Princeton: Princeton Univ. Press, 1978.

Bromfield, Louis. *Pleasant Valley*. New York: Harper, 1943.

Brown, Roger, and Albert Gilman. "The Pronouns of Power and Solidarity." In *Style in Language,* edited by Thomas A. Sebeok, 253–76. Cambridge: MIT Press, 1960.

Bryant, William Cullen. *Poems*. Oxford: Oxford Univ. Press, 1914.

Burchell, William J. *Travels in the Interior of Southern Africa* (1822). 2 vols. London: Batchworth, 1953.

Burke, Edmund. "On the Sublime and Beautiful." In *Essays*. London: Ward, Lock & Tyler, n.d.

Butler, Guy. *Selected Poems*. Johannesburg: Donker, 1975.

Butler, Guy, and Chris Mann, eds. *A New Book of South African Verse in English*. Cape Town: Oxford Univ. Press, 1979.

Campbell, John. *Travels in South Africa*. 3d ed. London, 1815.

Campbell, Roy. *Collected Works*. Vol. 1. Edited by Peter Alexander, Michael Chapman, and Marcia Leveson. Johannesburg: Donker, 1985.

Carter, A. E. *The Idea of Decadence in French Literature*. Toronto: Univ. of Toronto Press, 1950.

Cecil, Robert. *The Myth of the Master Race: Alfred Rosenberg and Nazi Ideology*. London: Batsford, 1972.

Clark, Kenneth. *Landscape into Art*. London: Murray, 1945.

Clouts, Sydney. *Collected Poems*. Cape Town: David Philip, 1984.

Coetzee, Abel. *C. M. van den Heever: Die wese van sy kuns*. Pretoria: Van Schaik, 1936.

Coleridge, Samuel Taylor. *Collected Works*. Vol. 1. Edited by Lewis Patton and Peter Mann. London: Routledge, 1971.

Crouch, Edward Heath, ed. *A Treasury of South African Poetry and Verse*. 2d ed. London: Fifield, 1909.

Damberger, C. F. *Travels in the Interior of Africa . . . 1781–97*. London, 1801.

Davis, David Brion. *The Problem of Slavery in Western Culture*. Ithaca: Cornell Univ. Press, 1966.

Deakin, Motley F., ed. *The Home Book of the Picturesque* (1852). Gainesville: Scholars' Facsimiles and Reprints, 1967.

De Grazia, Sebastian. *Of Time, Work and Leisure*. New York: Twentieth Century Fund, 1962.

Deleuze, Gilles. "*La Bête humaine:* Introduction." In *Zola,* edited by Colette Becker, 44–49. Paris: Garnier, 1972.

Delius, Anthony. *A Corner of the World.* Cape Town: Human & Rousseau, 1962.

De Man, Paul. "Intentional Structure of the Romantic Image." In *Romanticism and Consciousness,* edited by Harold Bloom. New York: Norton, 1970.

Dhlomo, H. I. E. *Collected Works.* Edited by Nick Visser and Tim Couzens. Johannesburg: Ravan, 1985.

Dover, Cedric. *Half-Caste.* London: Secker & Warburg, 1937.

Dugmore, H. H. *Verse.* Edited by E. H. Crouch. Cambridge, South Africa, 1920.

Eglington, Charles. *Under the Horizon.* Cape Town: Purnell, 1977.

Elphick, Richard. *Kraal and Castle: Khoikhoi and the Founding of White South Africa.* New Haven: Yale Univ. Press, 1977.

Emerson, Ralph Waldo. "Nature." In *The Portable Emerson,* edited by Carl Bode. Harmondsworth: Penguin, 1981.

Fairbridge, Kingsley. *Veld Verse.* Rev. ed. London: Oxford Univ. Press, 1928.

Foucault, Michel. *Madness and Civilization.* Translated by Richard Howard. New York: New American Library, 1967.

————. *Discipline and Punish.* Translated by Alan Sheridan. New York: Pantheon, 1977.

Fritsch, Gustav. *Drei Jahre in Süd-Afrika.* Breslau, 1868.

Gerwel, G. J. "Literatuur en apartheid: Konsepsies van 'gekleurdes' in die Afrikaanse roman tot 1948." Diss. Vrije Universiteit Brussel, 1979.

Gobineau, Arthur de. *Selected Political Writings.* Edited by Michael D. Biddiss. Translated by Adrian Collins. London: Cape, 1970.

Gordimer, Nadine. *The Conservationist.* London: Cape, 1974.

Haeckel, Ernst. *The History of Creation.* 8th ed. 2 vols. Translated by E. R. Lankester. London: Kegan Paul, 1906.

Hall, Thomas S. *Ideas of Life and Matter: Studies in the History of General Physiology.* Chicago: Univ. of Chicago Press, 1969.

Hanke, Lewis. *Aristotle and the American Indians.* Chicago: Regnery, 1959.

Haresnape, Geoffrey. *Pauline Smith.* New York: Twayne, 1969.

Harris, Marvin. *The Rise of Anthropological Theory.* London: Routledge, 1972.

Hawes, Louis. *The American Scene 1820–1900.* Bloomington: Indiana Univ. Art Museum, 1970.

Hawthorne, Nathaniel. *The Marble Faun.* New York: New American Library, 1961.

Hitler, Adolf. *Mein Kampf.* Translated by Ralph Manheim. London: Hutchinson, 1974.

Hondius, Jodocus. *A Clear Description of the Cape of Good Hope.* Translated by L. C. van Oordt. Cape Town: Van Riebeeck Festival Book Exhibition Committee, 1952.

Huntingdon, David C. *The Landscapes of Frederic Edwin Church.* New York: Braziller, 1966.

Hutt, W. H. *The Theory of Idle Resources.* London: Cape, 1939.

Ibsen, Henrik. *Ghosts.* Translated by Peter Watts. Harmondsworth: Penguin, 1964.

Irving, Washington. "A Tour on the Prairies." In *Selected Writings,* edited by William P. Kelly. New York: Modern Library, 1984.

Jones, Howard Mumford. *O Strange New World.* New York: Viking, 1964.

Jonker, Abraham H. *Die plaasverdeling.* Pretoria: Van Schaik, 1932.

———. *Die trekboer.* Bloemfontein: Nationale Pers Boekhandel, 1934.

Kannemeyer, J. C. *Geskiedenis van die Afrikaanse letterkunde.* Vol. 1. Cape Town: Academica, 1978.

Kant, Immanuel. *Critique of Aesthetic Judgment.* Edited and translated by James Creed Meredith. Oxford: Oxford Univ. Press, 1911.

Keith, W. J. *The Rural Tradition: A Study of the Non-Fiction Prose Writers of the English Countryside.* Toronto: Univ. of Toronto Press, 1974.

Kolb, Peter. *The Present State of the Cape of Good Hope.* Translated by Medley. 2 vols. London, 1731.

Kolodny, Annette. *The Lay of the Land.* Chapel Hill: Univ. of North Carolina Press, 1975.

Kroeber, Karl. *Romantic Landscape Vision: Constable and Wordsworth.* Madison: Univ. of Wisconsin Press, 1975.

Lawrence, D. H. *The Plumed Serpent.* London: Secker, 1926.

Lecky, William. *History of European Morals.* 2 vols. London, 1869.

Lee, Richard B. "What Hunters Do for a Living." In *Man the Hunter,* edited by Richard B. Lee and Irven DeVore, 30–48. Chicago: Aldine, 1968.

Leipoldt, C. Louis. *Versamelde gedigte.* Edited by J. C. Kannemeyer. Cape Town: Tafelberg, 1980.

Le Vaillant, François. *New Travels in the Interior Parts of Africa.* 3 vols. London, 1796.

Lewis, Meriwether, and William Clark. *Journals.* Edited by Bernard DeVoto. Boston: Houghton Mifflin, 1953.

Lewis, R. W. B. *The American Adam.* Chicago: Univ. of Chicago Press, 1955.

L'Honoré Naber, S. P., ed. *Reisebeschreibungen von deutschen Beamten und Kriegsleuten im Dienst der Niederländischen West- und Ost-Indischen Kompagnien, 1702–97.* Vol. 7. The Hague: Nijhoff, 1931.

Lipson, E. *The Growth of English Society.* 2d ed. London: Black, 1951.

Louw, N. P. van Wyk. *Versamelde gedigte.* Cape Town: Tafelberg, 1981.

Macfarlane, Alan. *The Origins of English Individualism.* Oxford: Blackwell, 1978.

Malherbe, D. F. *Die meulenaar.* Bloemfontein: Nasionale Pers, 1926.

Marais, J. S. *The Cape Coloured People, 1652–1937.* Johannesburg: Witwatersrand Univ. Press, 1957.

Marcus, Hugo. "Die Distanz in der Landschaft." *Zeitschrift für Aesthetik und allgemeine Kunstwissenschaft* 11 (1916):46–60.

Marinelli, Peter V. *Pastoral.* London: Methuen, 1971.

Marsh, Jan. *Back to the Land.* London: Quartet, 1982.

Marx, Karl. "Economic and Philosophic Manuscripts of 1844." In Karl Marx and Friedrich Engels, *Works,* vol. 3, translated by Clemens Dutt, 229–346. London: Lawrence & Wishart, 1975.

Mentzel, O. F. *A Geographical and Topographical Description of the Cape of Good Hope.* Translated by G. V. Marais and J. Hoge. Edited H. J. Mandelbrote. 2 vols. Cape Town: Van Riebeeck Society, 1944.

Mikro [C. H. Kühn]. *Toiings.* 1934. Reprint. Pretoria: Van Schaik, 1957.

———. *Pelgrims.* Pretoria: Van Schaik, 1935.

———. *Vreemdelinge.* Johannesburg: Afrikaanse Pers Boekhandel, 1944.

———. *Huisies teen die heuwel.* Cape Town: Nasionale Pers, 1942.

Millin, Sarah Gertrude. *Adam's Rest.* London: Collins, 1922.

———. *The Coming of the Lord.* London: Constable, 1928.

———. *The Fiddler.* London: Constable, 1929.

———. *God's Step-Children.* 2d ed. London: Constable, 1951.

———. *The Herr Witchdoctor.* London: Heinemann, 1941.

———. *King of the Bastards.* London: Heinemann, 1950.

———. *The South Africans.* London: Constable, 1926.

————. *The Wizard Bird*. London: Heinemann, 1962.

Moodie, Donald, ed. and trans. *The Record; or a Series of Official Papers relative to the Condition and Treatment of the Native Tribes of South Africa.* Cape Town: Balkema, 1960.

Moodie, J. W. D. *Ten Years in South Africa*. 2 vols. London, 1835.

Mosse, George L. *The Crisis of German Ideology: Intellectual Origins of the Third Reich.* London: Weidenfeld & Nicolson, 1966.

Nienaber, P. J., ed. *Gedenkboek C. M. van den Heever, 1902–57.* Johannesburg: Afrikaanse Pers Boekhandel, 1959.

Novak, Barbara. *American Painting of the Nineteenth Century.* New York: Praeger, 1969.

Noyes, Russell. *Wordsworth and the Art of Landscape.* Bloomington: Indiana Univ. Press, 1968.

Nye, Robert A. "Sociology and Degeneration: The Irony of Progress." In *Degeneration: The Dark Side of Progress,* edited by J. Edward Chamberlin and Sander L. Gilman, 49–71. New York: Columbia Univ. Press, 1985.

Opperman, D. J., ed. *Groot verseboek.* 9th ed. Cape Town: Tafelberg, 1983.

Paterson, William. *Narrative of Four Journeys into the Country of the Hottentots, and Caffraria, 1777–79.* London, 1789.

Paton, Alan. *Cry, the Beloved Country.* New York: Scribner's, 1948.

Paulson, Ronald. *Literary Landscape: Turner and Constable.* New Haven: Yale Univ. Press, 1982.

Percival, Robert. *An Account of the Cape of Good Hope.* London, 1804.

Philip, John. *Researches in South Africa.* 2 vols. London, 1828.

Plomer, William. *Collected Poems.* London: Cape, 1960.

Poggioli, Renato. *The Oaten Flute.* Cambridge: Harvard Univ. Press, 1975.

Povey, John. "Landscape in Early South African Poetry." In *Olive Schreiner and After,* edited by Malvern van Wyk Smith and Don McLennan. Cape Town: David Philip, 1983.

Pringle, Thomas. *Narrative of a Residence in South Africa.* Edited by A. M. Lewin Robinson. Cape Town: Struik, 1966.

————. *Poems Illustrative of South Africa.* Edited by J. R. Wahl. Cape Town: Struik, 1970.

————. *Poetical Works.* London, 1839.

Queraldo Moreno, Ramón-Jesús. *El pensamiento filosófico-político de Bartolomé de las Casas.* Seville: Univ. of Seville, 1976.

Raven-Hart, R. *Before Van Riebeeck: Callers at South Africa from 1488 to 1652.* Cape Town: Struik, 1967.

————. *Cape Good Hope 1652–1702: The First Fifty Years of Dutch Colonisation as Seen by Callers.* 2 vols. Cape Town: Balkema, 1971.

Ricoeur, Paul. *The Symbolism of Evil.* Translated by Emerson Buchanan. New York: Harper & Row, 1967.

Rose, Cowper. *Four Years in Southern Africa.* London, 1829.

Rousseau, Jean-Jacques. *The Social Contrast and Discourses.* Translated by G. D. H. Cole. London: Dent, 1913.

Rubin, Martin. *Sarah Gertrude Millin: A South African Life.* Johannesburg: Donker, 1977.

Sahlins, Marshall. *Stone Age Economics.* London: Tavistock, 1974.

Sanford, Charles L. *The Quest for Paradise.* Urbana: Univ. of Illinois Press, 1961.

Schapera, Isaac, ed. and trans. *The Early Cape Hottentots.* Cape Town: Van Riebeeck Society, 1933.

Schreiner, Olive. *The Story of an African Farm.* 1883. Reprint. Harmondsworth: Penguin, 1979.

Schweizer, Gerhard. *Bauernroman und Faschismus.* Tubingen: Schloss, 1976.

Shanin, Teodor, ed. *Peasants and Peasant Societies.* Harmondsworth: Penguin, 1971.

Sinclair, F. D. *The Cold Veld.* Wynberg: Rustica, 1945.

Slater, Francis Carey. *Collected Poems.* Edinburgh: Blackwood, 1957.

————, ed. *A Centenary Book of South African Verse.* London: Longmans, 1925.

Slotkin, J. S. *Readings in Early Anthropology.* London: Methuen, 1965.

Smith, Pauline. *The Little Karoo.* 1925; rev. ed. 1930. Reprint. London: Cape, 1952.

————. *The Beadle.* London: Cape, 1926.

Sparrman, Anders. *A Voyage to the Cape of Good Hope . . . 1772–76.* Edited by V. S. Forbes. Translation revised by J. and I. Rudner. Cape Town: Van Riebeeck Society, 1975.

Spencer, Herbert. *On Social Evolution: Selected Writings.* Edited by J. D. Y. Peel. Chicago: Univ. of Chicago Press, 1972.

Stavorinus, J. C. *Reise nach dem Vorgebürge der guten Hoffnung, Java und Bengalen in den Jahren 1768 bis 1771.* Translated by Leuder. Berlin, 1796.

Steiner, George. *In Bluebeard's Castle.* London: Faber, 1971.

Stepan, Nancy. "Biology and Degeneration: Races and Proper Places." In *Degeneration: The Dark Side of Progress,* edited by J. Edward Chamberlin and Sander L. Gilman, 97–120. New York: Columbia Univ. Press, 1985.

Streuvels, Stijn. *De vlaschaard. Volledige werken,* vol. 6. Amsterdam: Wereldbibliotheek, 1954.

Sturt, George ["George Bourne"]. *Change in the Village.* 1912. Reprint. New York: Kellog, 1969.

———. *A Farmer's Life.* 1922. Reprint. London: Cape, 1927.

Swart, Koenraad W. *The Sense of Decadence in Nineteenth-Century France.* The Hague: Nijhoff, 1964.

Thacker, Christopher. *The Wildness Pleases: The Origins of Romanticism.* Beckenham: Croom Helm, 1983.

Thirsk, Joan. "The European Debate on Customs of Inheritance, 1500–1700." In *Family and Inheritance: Rural Society in Western Europe, 1200–1800,* edited by Jack Goody, Joan Thirsk, E. P. Thompson. Cambridge: Cambridge Univ. Press, 1976.

Thomsen, Hans. *Die Verteilung des landwirtschaftlichen Grundbesitzes in Südafrika.* Jena: Gustav Fischer, 1927.

Thoreau, Henry D. *Walden.* Edited by J. Lyndon Shanley. Princeton: Princeton Univ. Press, 1973.

Tichi, Cecilia. *New World, New Earth.* New Haven: Yale Univ. Press, 1979.

Valentijn, François. *Description of the Cape of Good Hope with the Matters Concerning It.* Vol. 2. Edited by E. H. Raidt. Translated by R. Raven-Hart. Cape Town: Van Riebeeck Society, 1975.

Van Bruggen, Jochem. *Ampie,* pt. I (1924), pt. II (1928), pt. III (1942). *Ampie: Die trilogie.* Johannesburg: Afrikaanse Pers Boekhandel, 1965.

Van den Heever, C. M. *Die Afrikaanse gedagte.* Pretoria: Van Schaik, 1935.

———. "Daiel se afskeid." *Versamelde werke.* Vol. 2.

———. *Droogte.* Pretoria: Van Schaik, 1930.

———. *Gister.* Bloemfontein: Nasionale Pers, 1941.

———. *Groei. Versamelde werke.* Vol. 6.

————. *Laat vrugte*. Bloemfontein: Nasionale Pers Boekhandel, 1939.

————. *Langs die grootpad. Versamelde werke.* Vol. 5.

————. *Op die plaas*. Bloemfontein: Nasionale Pers, 1927.

————. *Somer. Versamelde werke.* Vol. 3.

————. *Versamelde gedigte*. Pretoria: Van Schaik, 1945.

————. *Versamelde werke.* 6 vols. Johannesburg: Afrikaanse Pers Boekhandel, 1957.

Van der Merwe, P. J. *Trek: Studies oor die mobiliteit van die pioniersbevolking aan die Kaap.* Cape Town: Nasionale Pers, 1945.

Van Melle, Johannes. *Dawid Booysen.* Pretoria: Van Schaik, 1933.

Van Riebeeck, Jan. *Journals.* Edited by H. B. Thom, W. P. L. van Zyl, et al. 3 vols. Cape Town: Balkema, 1952.

Virgil. *Georgics.* Translated by Smith Palmer Bovie. Chicago: Univ. of Chicago Press, 1956.

Vontobel, Klara. *Das Arbeitsethos des deutschen Protestantismus.* Bern: Francke, 1946.

Voss, A. E. "A Generic Approach to the South African Novel in English." *University of Cape Town Studies in English* 7 (1977): 110–19.

————. "Die pêrels van Pauline or, The History of Smith." *English in Africa* 11 (1984): 107–17.

Wade, Michael. "Myth, Truth and the South African Reality in the Fiction of Sarah Gertrude Millin." *Journal of Southern African Studies* 1 (1974): 91–108.

Watson, J. R. *Picturesque Landscape and English Romantic Poetry.* London: Hutchinson, 1970.

Weber, Max. *The Protestant Ethic and the Spirit of Capitalism.* Translated by Talcott Parsons. London: Allen & Unwin, 1976.

Weinrich, Max. *Hitler's Professors.* New York: Yiddish Scientific Institute, 1946.

Weiskel, Thomas. *The Romantic Sublime.* Baltimore: Johns Hopkins Univ. Press, 1976.

Whitman, Walt. "Song of Myself." In *Leaves of Grass,* edited by Sculley Bradley and Harold W. Blodgett. New York: Norton, 1973.

Wilcocks, R. W., ed. *Carnegie Commission of Investigation: The Poor White Problem in South Africa: A Report.* Vol. 2, *The Poor White.* Stellenbosch: Pro-Ecclesia, 1932.

Williams, George H. *Wilderness and Paradise in Christian Thought.* New York: Harper & Row, 1962.

Williams, Raymond. *The Country and the City*. London: Chatto & Windus, 1973.

Wolf, Bryan Jay. *Romantic Re-Vision: Culture and Consciousness in Nine-teenth-Century American Painting and Literature*. Chicago: Univ. of Chicago Press, 1982.

Wordsworth, William. *A Guide through the District of the Lakes*. In *Prose Works*. Vol. 2. Edited by W. J. B. Owen and Jane Worthington Smyser. Oxford: Oxford Univ. Press, 1974.

————. *Poetical Works*. [Vol. 1]. Edited by E. de Selincourt. Oxford: Oxford Univ. Press, 1940.

————. *The Prelude*. Edited by Jonathan Wordsworth, M. H. Abrams, and Stephen Gill. New York: Norton, 1979.

Wright, David. *A South African Album*. Cape Town: David Philip, 1976.

Wright, Lewis B., ed. *The Elizabethans' America*. Cambridge: Harvard Univ. Press, 1965.

Zimmermann, Peter. *Der Bauernroman: Antifeudalismus, Konservatismus, Faschismus*. Stuttgart: Metzler, 1975.

Zola, Emile. *Nana. Les Rougon-Macquart*. Edited by Armand Lanoux and Henri Mitterand. Vol. 2. Paris: Gallimard, 1961.

Index